The Facts on Aging Quiz

2nd Edition

Erdman B. Palmore, Ph.D., was born in Japan of missionary parents and was raised in Virginia. He received a B.A. from Duke University, an M.A. from the University of Chicago, and a Ph.D. from Columbia University, all in sociology. He taught at Finch College and Yale University and did research for the Social Security Administration before joining the faculty at Duke University in 1967. At Duke he has been coordinator for the Duke Longitudinal Studies and principal investigator of several research projects. He is now professor emeritus and a senior fellow at the Duke Center for the Study of Aging and Human Development. Dr. Palmore has written or edited 17 books including the *Normal Aging* series, *International Handbook on the Aged, Handbook on the Aged in the U.S., The Honorable Elders Revisited, Retirement: Causes and Consequences*, and *Ageism*, published by Springer Publishing Company. He has also written 25 chapters in other books and more than 80 articles in professional journals. He now writes a monthly column, "The Vintage Years," for the magazine *Fifty Plus*. His books and articles have received several awards. He is a fellow of both the American Sociological Society and the Gerontological Society of America and has served as president of the Southern Gerontological Society. His research and teaching interests include race relations, retirement, longevity, life satisfaction, health, and international gerontology.

The Facts on Aging Quiz

Second Edition

Erdman B. Palmore, PhD

Springer Publishing Company

Springer Publishing Company, Inc.
536 Broadway
New York, NY 10012-3955

Cover design by Janet Joachim
Acquisitions Editor: Bill Tucker
Production Editor: Kathleen Kelly

98 99 00 01 02/5 4 3 2 1

Library of Congress Cataloging-in-Publication Data

Palmore, Erdman Ballagh, 1930–
The facts on aging quiz / Erdman B. Palmore.—2nd ed.
p. cm.
Includes bibliographical references and index.
ISBN 0-8261-5771-8
1. Aging—Examinations, questions, etc. 2. Aging—Attitudes—Research—Methodology. 3. Gerontology—Research—Methodology.
I. Title.
QP86.P29 1998
612.6′7—dc21 98-20243
CIP

Printed in the United States of America

Contents

Foreword

Erdman B. Palmore is a distinguished colleague whose career in gerontology developed and flourished at the Duke University Center for the Study of Aging and Human Development, where he is a senior fellow. In this brief book, he reports on an unusually productive two-decade–long project, the Facts on Aging Quiz. This project, begun in 1976, has three characteristics that, although they occur together infrequently, warm a scholar's heart when they do combine. Via the Facts on Aging Quiz, Professor Palmore has (a) explored some important theoretical and methodological issues involved in assessing reliably the distribution of knowledge about growing old; (b) provided practical illustrations of how such an instrument can be used to stimulate interest in aging; and (c) illustrated how scholars can experience personal satisfaction in work that is both academically significant and socially useful. Professor Palmore set out to develop a brief, practical stimulus that would provoke group discussions about growing older and about older adults, and his quiz has apparently succeeded in doing just that for a wide variety of groups.

Evidence generated by use of the quiz, however, has also demonstrated a widespread ignorance about aging processes and aging people in the United States. Using research to document accurate generalizations about growing older is more difficult than one might expect, but Professor Palmore has demonstrated that establishing the reliability and validity of a brief quiz on aging is a rewarding as well as lengthy and demanding exercise.

The theoretical and practical significance of Palmore's Facts on Aging Quiz is a story that the numerous users of the quiz are in the best position to tell. So Professor Palmore allows the users—friends and critics alike—to tell their story in this book. (Friends outnumber critics considerably.) The quiz, first published in *The Gerontologist* in 1977, has generated the largest number of requests for permission to reprint in the history of that journal. Publications reporting uses and evaluations of uses of the quiz now number more than 150 and continue to appear.

These outcomes from Palmore's work over the past two decades are not at all bad for a scholar who set out simply to develop a quiz about aging intended to stimulate discussion. But beyond national and international recognition for his research in gerontology, Erdman Palmore is known by colleagues as a scholar who likes his work. His pleasure is most evident when he is pursuing an intellectually significant problem that also promises practical benefits such as increased professional and societal understanding of aging processes and of older adults.

This book will be appreciatively read by those who want systematic insight into what scholars from a variety of disciplines and what average citizens know about aging. It will also be appreciated by those who like the scholarly detective work involved in instrument construction and validation.

This Second Edition improves the First Edition in three ways: it includes multiple choice versions of the three quizzes; it updates the wording and documentation for the facts on aging; and it includes abstracts of approximately 60 new studies that have been published since the First Edition. I enjoyed reading this book, and I recommend it to you.

George L. Maddox, Ph.D.

Preface

I put together the first Facts on Aging Quiz in 1976 as a way of stimulating student interest in my course on "Social Aspects of Aging" at Duke University. I had searched the literature for a short quiz I could give my students to demonstrate to them that they had many misconceptions about aging and that there were a lot of interesting facts on aging of which they were unaware. To my surprise, I discovered that there was no short objective quiz about the facts on aging. I did find several tests or scales on aging, and a few had been published (Golde & Kogan, 1959; Kogan, 1961; Tuckman & Lorge, 1952). However, these tests all share the following disadvantages:

1. They are long (40 or 50 items that require several pages of print).
2. They confuse factual statements with attitudinal statements, all of which are arbitrarily scored as being "favorable" or "unfavorable." For example, Kogan's (1961) statement, "Most old people would prefer to continue working just as long as they can, rather than be dependent on anybody," is probably false, depending on what is meant by "working" and "dependent." In fact, most old people are content to be retired and dependent on their Social Security and other retirement income. Yet, a "disagree" response is scored as showing an "unfavorable" attitude toward the aged. Unfortunately, some "negative stereotypes" about the aged are generally true, and some of the "positive" statements are generally false.

3. They do not document the factual statements, and we have nothing but the author's assertion that they are true or false. So I designed the first Facts on Aging Quiz (FAQ1) to avoid these disadvantages. It is short, containing 25 items requiring only one page and less than 5 minutes to complete. It is confined to factual statements that can be documented by empirical research. It is designed to cover the basic physical, mental, and social facts and the most common misconceptions about aging. In addition, it can be self-scored.

When I tried it out on my students, they responded so favorably that I proceeded to try it out on other classes and on fellows and faculty. The results were so encouraging that I submitted a revised version and its documentation and uses for publication in *The Gerontologist* (Palmore, 1977). Soon requests for permission to use the quiz in various studies and publications came pouring in. It became apparent that the quiz was satisfying a need felt by many gerontologists and others.

Several researchers followed my suggestion of using the quiz to measure the effects of lectures, courses, and other training experiences by comparing before and after scores. It occurred to me, however, that it would be preferable to have alternative forms for measuring knowledge before and after a training experience, so that the results would not be confused by the "practice effects" of using the same form twice. This led to the development of the second Facts on Aging Quiz (FAQ2). The FAQ2 can be used for the other purposes as well, which are described in Chapter 4. A third quiz, the Facts on Aging and Mental Health Quiz (FAMHQ), is presented in Chapter 3.

The most recent development is the publication of multiple-choice versions of the FAQ1 and FAQ2 (see Chapters 1 and 2). We found that the multiple-choice versions are more reliable than the true-false versions because multiple choice reduces the chances of guessing correctly.

As this book demonstrates, there are now more than 150 known studies using these quizzes, and dozens of journals, books, newsletters, newspapers, and other publications have reprinted some or all of the FAQ. The permissions editor at *The Gerontologist* has informed me that they have received more requests to reprint the FAQ1 than they have received for any other article. There has even been a videotape series produced on the FAQ1 (Courtenay & Suhart, 1980). The quizzes remain the only published tests of general knowledge about aging that are both short and whose validity is documented. (The Knowledge of Aging and the Elderly (KAE) is patterned after the FAQ, but it contains several errors and dubious assumptions. See Palmore, 1990.) In addition to providing updated and revised versions of the FAQs (including the multiple-choice versions) and the FAMHQ, the purposes of this edition are (a) to provide comprehensive instructions for the several quiz uses, (b) to discuss their various uses, (c) to examine their reliability and validity, (d) to provide the results of the many studies that have used the quizzes, and (e) to discuss possible future research using them. This book is designed to be useful to those who want to use the quizzes in their research, classes, lectures, or workshops; to those who are interested in levels of knowledge about aging among various groups; and to those interested in the methodological problems of measuring knowledge about aging.

The book is organized to deal with these purposes in the order just listed. The first three chapters present revised versions of the FAQ1 and FAQ2 and the FAMHQ (including the new multiple-choice versions). Each quiz is followed by updated documentation that provides the evidence supporting each item.

Chapter 4 provides instructions on how to use the various quizzes, depending on the purpose at hand. It discusses using the quizzes to educate, through correcting misconceptions and stimulating discussion; to measure the effects of instruction, by using alternative forms of the quiz before and after the instruction; to test knowledge on an individual or group basis; to identify the most frequent misconceptions in a group and distinguish between misconceptions and ignorance; and to measure attitudes toward the aged, by computing a net bias score. It also presents an alternative combination of items called the Psychological Facts on Aging Quiz (PFAQ).

The results of the more than 150 known studies using the quizzes are summarized in Chapter 5. Chapter 6 presents an assessment of the uses of the quizzes based on a survey by Barresi and Brubaker (1979) of 25 quiz users. The last chapter draws conclusions based on the entire book and discusses promising types of future research. Comprehensive abstracts of all known studies using the quizzes are provided in Part II. There is also an index so that information on the various studies and their findings may be easily located. I would like to thank my colleagues who have made helpful suggestions for revisions of the FAQ, and the dozens of investigators who have used the FAQ to research knowledge about aging. Thanks are due to Bob McKinlay, who originally suggested the idea for this book. Diana Harris and Paul Changas did most of the work developing and testing the multiple-choice versions of the quizzes. I also wish to thank the Duke Center for the Study of Aging and Human Development, whose support has made this book possible.

I hope this book will be useful to researchers, gerontologists, and students interested in knowledge and attitudes about aging and the aged. I will be interested in any comments you have about this book and how it was useful or could be improved. If you do (or have done) research using these quizzes, I would like to have a report of your results for possible inclusion in future editions of this handbook. My address is Box 3003, Duke University Medical Center, Durham, NC 27710.

List of Tables

Part I

The Facts on Aging Quizzes: Purposes and Methods

1

The Facts on Aging Quiz: Part 1

This chapter presents the revised True-False version of the FAQ1 and the revised multiple-choice version of the FAQ1, followed by documentation of the correct answers. These revisions consider the suggestions of those who have used it in their research, such as Miller and Dodder (1980) and Courtenay and Weidmann (1985). However, some suggestions of Miller and Dodder (1980) were not accepted because they were not useful and changed the meaning of some of the items (Palmore, 1981b).

THE FAQ1 TEST ITEMS (TRUE-FALSE FORMAT)

Mark the statements "T" for true, "F" for false, or "?" for don't know.

1. The majority of old people (age 65+) are senile (have defective memory, are disoriented, or demented).
2. The five senses (sight, hearing, taste, touch, and smell) all tend to weaken in old age.
3. The majority of old people have no interest in, nor capacity for, sexual relations.
4. Lung vital capacity tends to decline in old age.
5. The majority of old people feel miserable most of the time.

6. Physical strength tends to decline in old age.
7. At least one tenth of the aged are living in long-stay institutions (such as nursing homes, mental hospitals, homes for the aged, etc.).
8. Aged drivers have fewer accidents per driver than those under age 65.
9. Older workers usually cannot work as effectively as younger workers.
10. Over three fourths of the aged are healthy enough to do their normal activities without help.
11. The majority of old people are unable to adapt to change.
12. Old people usually take longer to learn something new.
13. Depression is more frequent among the elderly than among younger people.*
14. Older people tend to react slower than younger people.
15. In general, old people tend to be pretty much alike.
16. The majority of old people say they are seldom bored.
17. The majority of old people are socially isolated.
18. Older workers have fewer accidents than younger workers.
19. Over 20% of the population are now age 65 or over.
20. The majority of medical practitioners tend to give low priority to the aged.
21. The majority of old people have incomes below the poverty line (as defined by the federal government).
22. The majority of old people are working or would like to have some kind of work to do (including housework and volunteer work).
23. Old people tend to become more religious as they age.
24. The majority of old people say they are seldom irritated or angry.
25. The health and economic status of old people will be about the same or worse in the year 2010 (compared with younger people).

(Key to scoring: all the odd-numbered items are false, and all the even-numbered are true.)

---

* This item on depression is a replacement for the original Item 13 ("It is almost impossible for the average old person to learn something new") because of the similarity between the original item and Item 12.

FAQ1 MULTIPLE-CHOICE FORMAT

Note that this version of the multiple-choice format changes the wording and correct answers to some of the items compared with the original 1996 version (Harris, Changas, & Palmore, 1996). The key to the symbols (+, –, *) is given at the end of this quiz. (Do not include the symbols in the form given the students.)

Instructions: Circle the letter of the best answer. If you do not know the best answer, you may put a question mark to the left of the answers instead of circling a letter.

1. The proportion of people over 65 who are senile (have impaired memory, disorientation, or dementia) is
   a. About 1 in 100 +
   b. About 1 in 10 *
   c. About 1 in 2 –
   d. The majority –
2. The senses that tend to weaken in old age are
   a. Sight and hearing +
   b. Taste and smell +
   c. Sight, hearing, and touch +
   d. All five senses *
3. The majority of old couples
   a. Have little or no interest in sex –
   b. Are not able to have sexual relations –
   c. Continue to enjoy sexual relations *
   d. Think sex is for only the young –
4. Lung vital capacity in old age
   a. Tends to decline *
   b. Stays the same among nonsmokers +
   c. Tends to increase among healthy old people +
   d. Is unrelated to age +
5. Happiness among old people is
   a. Rare –
   b. Less common than among younger people –
   c. About as common as among younger people *
   d. More common than among younger people +

6. Physical strength
   a. Tends to decline with age *
   b. Tends to remain the same among healthy old people +
   c. Tends to increase among healthy old people +
   d. Is unrelated to age +
7. The percentage of people over 65 in long-stay institutions (such as nursing homes, mental hospitals, and homes for the aged) is about
   a. 5% *
   b. 10% –
   c. 25% –
   d. 50% –
8. The accident rate per driver over age 65 is
   a. Higher than for those under 65 –
   b. About the same as for those under 65 –
   c. Lower than for those under 65 *
   d. Unknown 0
9. Most workers over 65
   a. Work less effectively than younger workers –
   b. Work as effectively as younger workers *
   c. Work more effectively than younger workers +
   d. Are preferred by most employers +
10. The proportion of people over 65 who are able to do their normal activities is
    a. One tenth –
    b. One quarter –
    c. One half –
    d. More than three fourths *
11. Adaptability to change among people over 65 is
    a. Rare –
    b. Present among about half –
    c. Present among most *
    d. More common than among younger people +
12. As for old people learning new things
    a. Most are unable to learn at any speed –
    b. Most are able to learn, but at a slower speed *
    c. Most are able to learn as fast as younger people +
    d. Learning speed is unrelated to age +

13. Depression is more frequent among
    a. People over 65 –
    b. Adults under 65 *
    c. Young people 0
    d. Children 0
14. Old people tend to react
    a. Slower than younger people *
    b. At about the same speed as younger people +
    c. Faster than younger people +
    d. Slower or faster than others, depending on the type of test +
15. Old people tend to be
    a. More alike than younger people –
    b. As alike as younger people 0
    c. Less alike than younger people +
    d. More alike in some respects and less alike in others *
16. Most old people say
    a. They are seldom bored *
    b. They are usually bored –
    c. They are often bored –
    d. Life is monotonous –
17. The proportion of old people who are socially isolated is
    a. Almost all –
    b. About half –
    c. Less than a fourth *
    d. Almost none +
18. The accident rate among workers over 65 tends to be
    a. Higher than among younger workers –
    b. About the same as among younger workers –
    c. Lower than among younger workers *
    d. Unknown because there are so few workers over 65 –
19. The proportion of the U.S. population now age 65 or over is
    a. 3% 0
    b. 13% *
    c. 23% 0
    d. 33% 0
20. Medical practitioners tend to give older patients:
    a. Lower priority than younger patients *
    b. The same priority as younger patients +

c. Higher priority than younger patients +
d. Higher priority if they have Medicaid +

21. The poverty rate (as defined by the federal government) among old people is
    a. Higher than among children under age 18 –
    b. Higher than among all persons under 65 –
    c. About the same as among persons under 65 –
    d. Lower than among persons under 65 *
22. Most old people are
    a. Still employed +
    b. Employed or would like to be employed +
    c. Employed, do housework or volunteer work, or would like to do some kind of work *
    d. Not interested in any work –
23. Religiosity tends to
    a. Increase in old age 0
    b. Decrease in old age 0
    c. Be greater in the older generation than in the younger *
    d. Be unrelated to age 0
24. Most old people say they
    a. Are seldom angry *
    b. Are often angry –
    c. Are often grouchy –
    d. Often lose their tempers –
25. The health and economic status of old people (compared with younger people) in the year 2010 will
    a. Be higher than now *
    b. Be about the same as now –
    c. Be lower than now –
    d. Show no consistent trend –

Key:

* = Correct answer
\+ = Positive bias
– = Negative bias
0 = Neutral

DOCUMENTATION OF FAQ1 ITEMS

1. False. The majority of people aged 65 or over are not senile; that is, they do not have defective memories, nor are they disoriented or demented. In the United States, community surveys have indicated that about 10% of the elderly suffer from some form of dementia or severe mental illness (Gurland, 1995). Another 10% have mild to moderate mental impairment; but the majority are without impairment. In fact, fewer of the elderly have mental impairments than do younger persons (Myers et al., 1984). Most studies of short-term memory agree that there is little or no decline in everyday short-term memory ability of normally aging adults (Kausler, 1995). As for long-term memory, various community surveys have found that only about 10% of the aged cannot remember such things as the past president of the United States; their correct age, birth date, telephone number, mother's maiden name, or address; and the meaning of ordinary words. Thus, it is clear that most do not have such serious memory defects.

2. True. All five senses do tend to decline in old age. Most studies of taste and smell show that taste and odor sensitivity decrease with age, although some of these decreases may be the result of other factors, such as disease, drugs, and smoking (Schiffman, 1995). Nearly all studies of touch, hearing, and vision agree that these senses tend to decline in old age (Atchley, 1996).

3. False. The majority of persons past age 65 continue to have both interest in and capacity for sexual relations (Starr, 1995). The Duke Longitudinal Studies (Palmore, 1981c) found that sex continues to play an important role in the lives of the majority of men and women through the seventh decade of life. Most elderly report that sex after age 60 is as satisfying or more satisfying than when they were younger.

4. True. Lung vital capacity does tend to decline in old age. Forced vital capacity (the volume of air that can be forcibly expelled in one breath) tends to decline about 3 or 4 deciliters per decade, regardless of whether measured longitudinally or cross-sectionally (Pierce, 1995). This decline is even greater for smokers.

5. False. The majority of old people do not feel miserable most of the time. Studies of happiness, morale, and life satisfaction either find no significant difference by age group or find about one fifth to one third of the aged score "low" on various happiness or morale scales (Okun, 1995; Palmore, 1981c). A national survey found only one-fourth of persons age 65 or over reporting that "This is the dreariest time of my life," whereas about half said, "I am just as happy as when I was younger," and one third even said, "These are the best years of my life" (Harris, 1981).

6. True. Physical strength does tend to decline in old age. Physiological, biochemical, anatomic, and histocytological measurements of muscle all exhibit decreased levels with age from about the third decade. About one third of the muscle mass is usually lost by age 80 (Tonna, 1995).

7. False. Only 5% of persons aged 65 or over are residents of any long-stay institution at any one time (Kahana, 1995). Even among those aged 75 or over, only 9% are residents of institutions. However, about 40% of the elderly spend time in a nursing home at some point in their lives.

8. True. Drivers age 65 or over do have fewer accidents per driver than drivers under age 65. Older drivers have about the same accident rate per 100 persons as middle-aged drivers (13) but a much lower rate than drivers under age 30 (National Safety Council, 1996). Older drivers tend to drive fewer miles per year and apparently compensate for declines in perception and reaction speed by driving more carefully (Hogue, 1995).

9. False. The majority of older workers can work as effectively as younger workers. Despite declines in perception and reaction speed under laboratory conditions among the general aged population, studies of employed older persons under actual working conditions generally show that they perform as well as, if not better than, younger workers on most measures (Rix, 1995). When speed and accuracy of movement are important to the job, some studies indicate decline with age (Rhodes, 1983). However, intellectual performance, on which much of work performance depends, does not decline substantially until the 70s in most individuals and even later in others (Labouvie-Vief, 1985). Consistency of output tends to increase with age, and older workers have less job turnover, fewer accidents, and less absenteeism than younger workers.

10. True. More than 85% of the aged are healthy enough to engage in their basic activities of daily living, such as eating, bathing, dressing, and so on (Wiener et al., 1990). About 5% of those 65 or over are institutionalized, and another 5% to 8% (depending on the survey) of the noninstitutionalized need help to engage in their activities of daily living.

11. False. The majority of older persons are able to adapt to change. It is clear that most older persons do change and adapt to the many changes that occur in old age, such as retirement, children leaving home, widowhood, moving to new homes, and serious illness. Their political and social attitudes also tend to shift with those of the rest of society and with approximately the same rate of change (Cutler, 1995).

12. True. Old people do usually take longer to learn something new compared with their own performances when they were younger or with performances of a younger cohort (Poon, 1995). However, much of these differences can be explained by variables other than age (e.g., illness, motivation, learning style, or lack of practice). When these other variables are taken into account, chronological age does not provide a significant amount of influence on learning ability.

13. False. Actually, major depression ("clinical depression") is less prevalent among the elderly than among younger persons. The National Institute of Mental Health surveys of three communities found that major depressive disorders (not counting bereavement) were less than half as prevalent among those over age 65 as in the general population (Myers et al., 1984).

14. True. The reaction time of most old people does tend to be slower than that of younger people. This is one of the best-documented facts about the aged. It appears to be true regardless of the kind of reaction that is measured (Cerella, 1995). However, the increased reaction time in the usual experiment is only a small fraction of a second, which does not prevent adequate performance in most ordinary activities.

15. False. Old people are not pretty much alike. There is at least as much variation among older people as there is at any age; there are the rich and poor, happy and sad, healthy and sick, and those of high and low intelligence. In fact, some evidence indicates that as people age they tend to become less alike and more heterogeneous on many dimensions (Palmore, 1981c).

16. True. The majority of old people do say they are seldom bored. Only 21% say that "Most of the things I do are boring or monotonous" (Harris, 1981), and only 17% say that "not enough to do to keep busy" is a problem for them. The Duke Second Longitudinal Study of Aging

(Palmore, 1981c) found that 87% said they had never been bored in the past week.

17. False. The majority of old people are not socially isolated. About two thirds live with their spouse or family (Coward & Netzer, 1995). Only about 4% of the elderly are extremely isolated, and most of these have had lifelong histories of withdrawal (Kahana, 1995). Most elders have close relatives within easy visiting distance, and contacts between them are relatively frequent.

18. True. Older workers do have fewer accidents than younger workers (Root, 1981), probably because they tend to avoid dangerous situations and hazardous jobs.

19. False. Only 12.8% of the U.S. population were age 65 or over in 1997, although this may increase to 21% by the year 2040 (U.S. Bureau of the Census, 1993).

20. True. The majority of medical practitioners do tend to give low priority to the aged. All studies of attitudes toward the aged among medical and human service professionals agree that they tend to believe the negative stereotypes about the aged and prefer to work with children or younger adults rather than with the aged (Palmore, 1990). Few specialize in geriatrics or are interested in specializing in it. The aged are labeled resistant to treatment, rigid in outlook, senile, unreliable, and unable to learn new things or to change their ways.

21. False. The majority of persons aged 65 or over have incomes well above the poverty level. In 1994 only 10.5% of persons over 65 had incomes below the official poverty level (about $6,500 for an aged individual or $8,000 for an aged couple). This was a lower poverty rate than for adults under 65 (11.4%). The poverty rate for all persons under 65 was even higher: 13.8% (Baugher & Lamison-White, 1996). Even if the "near poor" (those with incomes up to 150% of the poverty level) are included, the total in or near poverty was only 29% (Hess & Markson, 1995).

22. True. Over three fourths of old people are working or would like to have some kind of work to do (including housework and volunteer work). About 7% of persons age 65 or older are employed, 21% are retired but say they would like to be employed, 17% work as homemakers, 19% are not employed but do volunteer work, and another 9% are not employed or doing volunteer work but would like to do volunteer work (Harris, 1981).

23. False. Older people do not tend to become more religious as they age. Although it is true that the present generation of older persons tends to be more religious than the younger generations, this appears to be a generational difference (rather than an aging effect) because of the older persons' more religious upbringing. In other words, members of the present older generation have been more religious all their lives rather than becoming more religious as they aged (Blazer & Palmore, 1976; Levin, 1995).

24. True. The majority of old people do say they are seldom irritated or angry. The Duke Second Longitudinal Study (Palmore, 1981c) found that 90% of persons age 65 or older said they were never angry during the past week. Self-reports of anger tend to decrease in old age (Barefoot, 1995).

25. False. The health and economic status of old people (compared with younger people) in the year 2010 will probably be much higher than now. Measures of health, income, occupation, and education among older people are all rising in comparison with those of younger people. In other words, the gaps between older and younger people on these dimensions will probably be substantially less (Clark, 1995; Manton, 1995; Palmore, 1986; Peterson, 1995). This reduction in gaps is largely due to improvements in health, income, occupation, and education among the younger cohorts now moving into the 65 and older category.

2

The Facts on Aging Quiz: Part 2

This chapter provides a revised version of the FAQ2 and a revised multiple-choice version, followed by updated documentation on the correct answers. Note that Item 21 has been changed from the original version ("About 3% more of the aged have incomes below the official poverty level than the rest of the population"), which is no longer true, to a currently true statement ("The aged have a lower rate of poverty than the rest of the population").

THE FAQ2 TEST ITEMS (TRUE-FALSE FORMAT)

Mark the statements "T" for true, "F" for false, or "?" for don't know.

1. A person's height tends to decline in old age.
2. More older persons (65 or older) have chronic illnesses that limit their activity than do younger persons.
3. Older persons have more acute (short-term) illnesses than do younger persons.
4. Older persons have more injuries in the home than younger persons.

5. Older workers have less absenteeism than do younger workers.
6. Blacks' life expectancy at age 65 is about the same as Whites'.
7. Men's life expectancy at age 65 is about the same as women's.
8. Medicare pays over half of the medical expenses for the aged.
9. Social Security benefits automatically increase with inflation.
10. Supplemental Security Income guarantees a minimum income for needy aged.
11. The aged do not get their proportionate share of the nation's income.
12. The aged have higher rates of criminal victimization than younger persons.
13. The aged are more fearful of crime than are younger persons.
14. The aged are the most law abiding of all adult age groups.
15. There are about equal numbers of widows and widowers among the aged.
16. More of the aged vote than any other age group.
17. There are proportionately more older persons in public office than in the total population.
18. The proportion of African Americans among the aged is growing.
19. Participation in voluntary organizations (churches and clubs) tends to decline even among the healthy aged.
20. The majority of old people live alone.
21. The aged have a lower rate of poverty than the rest of the population.
22. The rate of poverty among aged African Americans is about three times as high as among aged Whites.
23. Older persons who reduce their activity tend to be happier than those who do not.
24. When the last child leaves home, the majority of parents have serious problems adjusting to their "empty nest."
25. The proportion widowed among the aged is decreasing.

(Key: Alternating pairs of items are true or false; that is, 1 and 2 are true, 3 and 4 are false, 5 and 6 are true, and so forth, and 25 is true.)

FAQ2 MULTIPLE-CHOICE FORMAT

Note that this revised version changes some of the wording and correct answers compared with the original version (Harris & Changas, 1944). See key at end for meaning of the symbols after the options. (Do not include these symbols in the form given to students.)

Instructions: Circle the letter of the best answer. If you do not know the best answer, you may put a question mark (?) to the left of the answers instead of circling a letter.

1. In old age, a person's height
   a. Does not change +
   b. Only appears to change +
   c. Tends to decline *
   d. Depends on how active one is +
2. Compared with younger persons, more older persons (65 or over) are limited in their activity by which type of illnesses?
   a. Acute illnesses (short term) –
   b. Colds and flu –
   c. Infections –
   d. Chronic illnesses *
3. Which type of illness do older persons have less frequently than younger persons?
   a. Chronic illness +
   b. Arthritis +
   c. Stroke +
   d. Acute illness *
4. Compared with younger persons, older persons have
   a. More injuries in the home –
   b. About the same number of injuries in the home –
   c. Fewer injuries in the home *
   d. Twice the liklihood to be injured in the home –
5. Older workers' absenteeism rates
   a. Are higher than among younger workers –
   b. Cannot be trusted –
   c. Are about the same as among younger workers –
   d. Are lower than among younger workers *

6. The life expectancy of African Americans at age 65
   a. Is higher than that of whites 0
   b. Is lower than that of whites 0
   c. Is about the same as that of whites *
   d. Has not been determined 0
7. Men's life expectancy at age 65 compared with women's
   a. Is lower *
   b. Is dropping 0
   c. Is about the same 0
   d. Is higher 0
8. What percentage of medical expenses for the aged does Medicare pay?
   a. About 20 percent –
   b. About 45 percent *
   c. About 75 percent +
   d. Nearly 100 percent +
9. Social Security benefits
   a. Automatically increase with inflation *
   b. Are not subject to change –
   c. Must be adjusted by Congress –
   d. Are often cut back to balance the deficit –
10. Supplemental Security Income (SSI)
    a. Guarantees a minimum income for the needy elderly *
    b. Provides extra income for all elderly +
    c. Supplements the income of elderly in nursing homes +
    d. Pays medical expenses for the elderly +
11. As for income
    a. The majority of elderly live below the poverty level. –
    b. The elderly are the poorest age group in our society. –
    c. The elderly get their proportionate share of the nation's income. *
    d. The income gap between the elderly and younger people is widening. –
12. Compared with younger persons, rates of criminal victimization among the elderly are
    a. Higher –
    b. Lower *

c. About the same –
d. Steadily increasing –

13. Fear of crime among the elderly
    a. Is higher than among younger persons *
    b. Is about the same as among younger persons +
    c. Is lower than among younger persons +
    d. Is not significant +
14. The most law abiding adults are
    a. Those in their 20s –
    b. Those in their 30s –
    c. Those 45 to 65 –
    d. Those over 65 *
15. Comparing widows with widowers among the aged
    a. Their numbers are about equal. +
    b. There are about twice as many widows as widowers. +
    c. There are about five times as many widows as widowers. *
    d. There are about twice as many widowers as widows. +
16. Voter participation rates are usually
    a. Highest among those over 65 +
    b. Highest among those age 55 to 64 *
    c. Highest among those age 40 to 54 –
    d. Highest among those age 20 to 39 –
17. Being elected or appointed to public office is
    a. Rare among those over 65 –
    b. More frequent among those under 65 –
    c. More frequent among those over 65 *
    d. Similar in frequency among older and younger persons –
18. The proportion of African Americans among the aged is
    a. Growing *
    b. Declining 0
    c. Staying about the same 0
    d. Small compared with most other minority groups 0
19. Participation in voluntary organizations usually
    a. Does not decline among healthy older persons *
    b. Declines among healthy older persons –
    c. Increases among healthy older persons +
    d. Is highest among healthy youth –

20. The majority of old people live
    a. Alone –
    b. In long-stay institutions –
    c. With their spouses *
    d. With their children –
21. The rate of poverty among the elderly is
    a. Lower than among those under 65 *
    b. Higher than among those under 65 –
    c. The same as it is for other age groups –
    d. High as a result of their fixed incomes –
22. The rate of poverty among aged African Americans is
    a. Less than that of whites 0
    b. About the same as that of whites 0
    c. Double that of whites 0
    d. Almost triple that of whites *
23. Older persons who reduce their activity tend to be
    a. Happier than those who remain active –
    b. Not as happy as those who remain active *
    c. About as happy as others –
    d. Healthier –
24. When the last child leaves home, the majority of parents
    a. Have serious problems of adjustment –
    b. Have higher levels of life satisfaction *
    c. Try to get their children to come back home –
    d. Suffer from the "empty nest" syndrome –
25. The proportion widowed among the aged
    a. Is gradually decreasing *
    b. Is gradually increasing –
    c. Has remained the same in this century –
    d. Is unrelated to longevity –

Key:

* = Correct answer
\+ = Positive bias
– = Negative bias
0 = Neutral

DOCUMENTATION OF FAQ2 ITEMS

1. True. Height does tend to decline in old age. Cross-sectional studies of 35 different populations around the world all show that persons in each decade of life over 50 are shorter than the persons in the previous decade. Some of these differences are due to cohort (generational) differences because later cohorts have tended to be taller than earlier cohorts, presumably because of improved environmental conditions, such as nutrition. However, all the longitudinal studies (which repeatedly measure the same cohort over many years) also show decreases in average height after age 55 (Shock, 1985). This decrease in height appears to be mainly caused by changes in posture or "slump" and by decreases in the thickness of the intervertebral discs.

2. True. More older persons do have chronic illnesses that limit their activity (38%) than do younger persons (15%). The discrepancy is similar for the percentages with chronic illnesses that limit their major activity (National Center for Health Statistics, 1995).

3. False. The fact is that older persons have fewer acute illnesses than younger persons: In 1994 there were 110 acute illnesses per 100 persons over age 65 per year compared with 172 for all persons (National Center for Health Statistics, 1995). Thus, the higher rate of chronic illness among the aged is partially offset by the lower rate of acute illness.

4. False. Actually, older persons have fewer injuries in the home than do younger persons: 12.5 per 100 persons over 65 per year compared with 14 for persons under 65 (National Center for Health Statistics, 1995).

5. True. Most older workers do have less absenteeism than younger workers (Atchley, 1996). The only exceptions are unhealthy older workers.

6. True. African Americans' life expectancy at age 65 is about the same as Whites'. In 1994 the average 65-year-old White could expect to live another 17 years, whereas a 65-year-old African American could expect to live another 16 years (Anderson, Kochanek, Murphy, 1997).

7. False. The life expectancy of men at age 65 continues to be substantially less than that of women, just as it is at younger ages. In 1995, men's life expectancy at age 65 was 15 years, whereas women's was 19. (Anderson, Kochanek, & Murphy, 1997). However, this gap has decreased by 8% since 1970.

8. False. Medicare pays less than half of the medical expenses for the aged. In 1991 Medicare covered 45% of the personal health care expenditures of the aged (U.S. Senate Special Committee on Aging, 1991). Among the "medically indigent," Medicaid covered an additional 13%, and other public programs (such as the Veterans Administration) covered another 6%.

9. True. Social Security benefits do automatically increase with inflation. Since 1975, Social Security benefits have been automatically increased whenever the Consumer Price Index of the Bureau of Labor Statistics for the first calendar quarter of a year exceeds by at least 3% the index for the first quarter of the preceding year. The size of the benefit increase is determined by the actual percentage rise of the index during the quarters measured.

10. True. SSI does guarantee a minimum income for needy aged. In 1974, the SSI program was established to provide a minimum monthly income for all persons over 65 with assets of less than a stated amount ($2,000 for an individual and $3,000 for a couple in 1997), excluding the value of a home, household goods, personal effects, an automobile, life insurance of less than $1,500, and property needed for self-support. In 1997, persons over 65 could receive monthly payments of up to $484 for an individual or $726 for a couple. Some states also supplement these payments with an additional amount.

11. False. The aged do get their proportionate share of the nation's income. Although the adjusted after-tax mean income plus government transfers of households with members age 65 or over is only 82% of that of all households, this does not take into account the fact that older households tend to be smaller, so they need less income than the larger, younger households. Careful studies based on the construction of equivalence scales indicate that the incomes of older and younger households are now roughly comparable (Crown, 1995).

12. False. The aged actually have lower rates of criminal victimization than those under 65. Persons over 65 have lower victimization rates in nearly all categories of personal crime: rape, robbery, assault, and personal theft. The only category in which the rate for older persons is higher than that of younger persons is "personal larceny with contact" (which includes purse snatching and pickpocketing), and this category accounts for less than 3% of all personal crimes. When all personal crimes are added together, persons over 65 have a victimization rate that is less than one fourth that of all persons over age 12. Furthermore, violent crime, personal theft, and household crime victimization rates for older persons have been decreasing steadily over the past two decades (Cutler, 1995).

13. True. The aged are more fearful of crime, despite their lower chances of victimization. For example, a national survey (Harris, 1981) found that 25% of those 65 or over said that fear of crime was a "very serious" problem for them compared with 20% of those aged 18 to 64. Among the aged, fear of crime is even greater among women, Blacks, and residents of central cities (Atchley, 1996).

14. True. The aged are the most law abiding of all adult groups, regardless of how it is measured. For example, persons over age 65 have about one tenth as high an arrest rate for all offenses as the arrest rate for all ages. (Atchley, 1996). Similarly, persons aged 65 or over are incarcerated in prisons and jails at about one tenth the overall rate.

15. False. There are almost five times as many widows as widowers among the aged (U.S. Senate Special Committee on Aging, 1991). This is the result of several factors: Women tend to marry men older than themselves, women tend to live longer than men, and widows do not remarry as often as do widowers, partly because of the scarcity of eligible widowers.

16. False. Persons over 65 vote less often than do those age 55 to 64. For the past 20 years in national elections voters age 55 to 64 always had higher participation rates than those 65 and over (U.S. Senate Special Committee on Aging, 1991). However, sometimes the "young-old" (those aged 65–74) had a higher voting rate than those aged 55–64. Furthermore, it appears that the lower voting participation of the aged is not due to aging processes, but to the larger proportions of the aged who are female and have less education.

17. True. There are proportionately more older persons in public office, and this is even more true of the higher officials. The generally positive relationship between old age and high political office is found throughout history and across types of political systems (Atchley, 1996).

18. True. The proportion of African Americans among the aged is growing. In 1960 African Americans were 6% of all persons aged 65 or over, and by 2000 this percentage will increase to 9% (U.S. Senate Special Committee on Aging, 1991). It is estimated that by 2025 about 14% of the aged will be African Americans.

19. False. Participation in voluntary organizations does not usually decline among healthy older persons. Several studies have shown that, when the effects of socioeconomic differences and health are controlled, age bears little or no relationship to voluntary association participation in middle age or later life (Cutler, 1995). However, illness does tend to decrease participation.

20. False. Two thirds of noninstitutionalized persons over 65 live in a family setting. Only 28% live alone (Coward & Netzer, 1995).

21. True. In 1995, 10.5% of persons age 65 or older were in poverty compared with 13.8% of all persons under age 65 (U.S. Bureau of the Census, 1997). Persons over 65 also had a slightly lower poverty rate than other adults (11.4%). The inclusion of children among those under 65 increases their poverty rate by about 2%.

22. True. The rate of poverty among aged African Americans is almost three times as high as among whites. In 1996 the poverty rate among African American elders was 25% compared with 9% for white elderly (Baugher & Lamison-White, 1996).

23. False. Older persons who disengage from active roles do not tend to be happier than those who remain active. On the contrary, most recent surveys and longitudinal studies have found that those who remain active tend to be happier than those who disengage, although some studies found no relationship between activity and happiness (Atchley, 1996; Larson, 1978).

24. False. When the last child leaves home, the majority of parents do not have serious problems adjusting to their "empty nest" (Atchley, 1996). In fact, the parents whose children have not left home tend to have lower life satisfaction and happiness (Palmore, Cleveland, Nowlin, Ramm, & Siegler, 1979).

25. True. The proportion widowed is gradually decreasing among the aged because of decreasing mortality rates (Myers, 1995). Apparently, increasing longevity increases the average age at widowhood and thus increases the proportion of years beyond age 65 in which the couple survives as a couple.

3

The Facts on Aging and Mental Health Quiz

This chapter presents a revised true-false version and a multiple-choice version (previously unpublished) of the quiz that deals with mental health and aging. This is an area of increasing concern for scientists, geropsychiatrists, and older persons and their families. This growing concern is based on the escalating costs of caring for mentally ill elders and the intensifying efforts to find preventions and cures, or at least effective treatments for the devastating effects of senile dementia and other mental illnesses among the aged. This quiz, which will be referred to as the FAMHQ, will be especially useful to health care workers and relatives of older persons with mental problems.

THE FAMHQ TEST ITEMS (TRUE-FALSE FORMAT)

Mark the following with a "T" for true, "F" for false, or "?" for don't know.

1. The majority of persons over 65 have some mental illness severe enough to impair their abilities.
2. Cognitive impairment (memory loss, disorientation, or confusion) is an inevitable part of the aging process.

3. If an older mental patient makes up false stories, it is best to point out that he or she is lying.
4. The prevalence of neurosis and schizophrenia increases in old age.
5. Suicide rates increase with age for women past 45.
6. Suicide rates increase with age for men past 45.
7. Fewer of the aged have mental impairments, when all types are added together, than other age groups.
8. The primary mental illness of the elderly is cognitive impairment.
9. Alzheimer's disease (progressive senile dementia) is the most common type of chronic cognitive impairment among the aged.
10. There is no cure for Alzheimer's disease.
11. Most patients with Alzheimer's disease act the same way.
12. Organic brain impairment is easy to distinguish from functional mental illness.
13. It is best not to look directly at older mental patients when you are talking to them.
14. It is best to avoid talking to demented patients because it may increase their confusion.
15. Demented patients should not be allowed to talk about their past because it may depress them.
16. The prevalence of cognitive impairment increases in old age.
17. Isolation and hearing loss are the most frequent causes of paranoid disorders in old age.
18. Poor nutrition may produce mental illness among the elderly.
19. Mental illness is more prevalent among the elderly with less income and education.
20. The majority of nursing home patients suffer from mental illness.
21. The elderly have fewer sleep problems than younger persons.
22. Major depression is more prevalent among the elderly than among younger persons.
23. Widowhood is more stressful for older than for younger women.
24. More of the aged use mental health services than do younger persons.
25. Psychotherapy is usually ineffective with older patients.

(Key: The items alternate being true or false in groups of five: The first five items are false; the next five (6–10) are true; and so on.)

FAMHQ MULTIPLE-CHOICE VERSION

Circle the letter of the most accurate answer. If you do not know, you may put a question mark to the left of the answers instead of circling a letter.

1. Severe mental illness among persons over 65 afflicts
   a. The majority –
   b. About half –
   c. About 15% to 25% *
   d. Very few +
2. Cognitive impairment (impairment of memory, disorientation, or confusion)
   a. Is an inevitable part of the aging process –
   b. Increases in old age *
   c. Declines with age +
   d. Does not change with age +
3. If older mental patients make up false stories, it is best to
   a. Point out to them that they are lying –
   b. Punish them for lying –
   c. Reward them for their imagination +
   d. Ignore or distract them *
4. The prevalence of anxiety disorders and schizophrenia in old age tends to
   a. Decrease *
   b. Stay about the same –
   c. Increase somewhat –
   d. Increase markedly –
5. Suicide rates among women tend to
   a. Increase in old age –
   b. Stay about the same *
   c. Decrease somewhat in old age +
   d. Decrease markedly +
6. Suicide rates among men tend to
   a. Increase markedly *
   b. Increase somewhat +
   c. Stay about the same +
   d. Decrease +

7. When all major types of mental impairment are added together, the elderly have
   a. Higher rates than younger persons –
   b. About the same rates as younger persons –
   c. Lower rates than younger persons *
   d. Higher rates for ages 65 to 74 than for those over 75 0
8. The primary mental illness of the elderly is
   a. Anxiety disorders +
   b. Mood disorders +
   c. Schizophrenia 0
   d. Cognitive impairment *
9. Alzheimer's disease is
   a. The most common type of cognitive impairment *
   b. An acute illness +
   c. A benign memory disorder +
   d. A form of affective disorder +
10. Alzheimer's disease usually
    a. Can be cured with psychotherapy +
    b. Can be cured with pharmacology +
    c. Goes into remission among the very old +
    d. Cannot be cured *
11. Most patients with Alzheimer's disease
    a. Act pretty much the same way –
    b. Have confusion and impaired memory *
    c. Wander during the day or at night –
    d. Repeat the same question or action over and over –
12. Organic brain impairment
    a. Is easy to distinguish from functional mental illness +
    b. Is difficult to distinguish from functional mental illness *
    c. Tends to be similar to functional mental illness +
    d. Can be reversed with proper therapy +
13. When talking to an older mental patient, it is best
    a. To avoid looking directly at the patient –
    b. To glance at the patient occasionally –
    c. To ignore the patient's reactions –
    d. To look directly at the patient *
14. Talking with demented older patients
    a. Tends to increase their confusion –
    b. Is usually pleasurable for the patient *

c. Should be confined to trivial matters –
d. Should be avoided as much as possible –

15. When demented patients talk about their past, it usually
    a. Is enjoyed by the patient *
    b. Depresses the patient –
    c. Increases the patient's confusion –
    d. Has no effect –
16. The prevalence of severe cognitive impairment
    a. Is unrelated to age +
    b. Decreases with age +
    c. Increases with age after age 45 *
    d. Increases with age only after age 75 +
17. The primary causes of paranoid disorders in old age are
    a. Isolation and hearing loss *
    b. Persecution and abuse 0
    c. Near death experiences 0
    d. None of the above 0
18. Poor nutrition may produce
    a. Depression 0
    b. Confusion 0
    c. Apathy 0
    d. All of the above *
19. Mental illness in elders is more prevalent among
    a. The poor *
    b. The rich 0
    c. The middle-class 0
    d. None of the above 0
20. The prevalence of mental illness among elderly in long-term care institutions is:
    a. About 10% +
    b. About 25% +
    c. About 50% +
    d. More than 75% *
21. Elders tend to have
    a. Less sleep problems +
    b. More sleep problems *
    c. Deeper sleep +
    d. The same sleep patterns as younger persons +

22. Major depression is
    a. Less prevalent among elders *
    b. More prevalent among elders –
    c. Unrelated to age –
    d. A sign of senility –
23. Widowhood is
    a. Less stressful among elders *
    b. More stressful among elders –
    c. Similar levels of stress at all ages –
    d. Least stressful among young adults –
24. Elders use mental health facilities
    a. More often than younger people –
    b. Less often than younger people *
    c. At about the same rate as younger people –
    d. Primarily when they have no family to care for them –
25. Psychotherapy with older patients is
    a. Usually ineffective –
    b. Often effective *
    c. Effective with Alzheimer's patients 0
    d. A waste of the therapist's time –

DOCUMENTATION OF FAMHQ ITEMS

1. False. The majority of persons over age 65 do not have any mental illness. The major community surveys have found from 65% to 82% of the aged to be mentally normal; only 15% to 25% are severely mentally ill (Gurland, 1995; U.S. Senate Special Committee on Aging, 1991).

2. False. Senile dementia is not an inevitable part of the aging process. Only 5% to 15% of persons over 65 have any kind of dementia (Gurland, 1995). However, among those over age 85, prevalence of severe dementia is estimated to be as high as 47% (U.S. Senate Special Committee on Aging, 1991).

3. False. Telling mental patients that they are lying is not an effective way of reducing false stories. Such patients are not usually "lying" in the sense of deliberate deception. They may be having a delusion or confusing their imagination with reality, or they may be attempting to fill in gaps in their memory. A better way of controlling such behavior is to ignore it, give a noncommittal answer, attempt to distract the person, or see if something in the environment can be changed to reduce confusion (Mace & Rabins, 1991).

4. False. The prevalence of anxiety disorders and schizophrenia does not increase but rather decreases in old age (Gurland, 1995). Apparently many persons with these illnesses either recover or do not survive to old age.

5. & 6. Item 5 is false, but 6 is true. Suicide rates do not increase with age among women, but they do increase markedly among men, doubling between the ages of 40 and 75 (Atchley, 1996). Older men tend to use more violent and successful forms of suicide, such as gunshot, whereas women have more attempted suicides that are unsuccessful.

7. True. Community studies sponsored by the National Institute on Mental Health (NIMH) in New Haven, Baltimore, Durham, and St. Louis all found that persons over 65 had the lowest overall prevalence rates of mental impairment when the eight most common disorders were grouped together (affective disorders, panic and obsessive/compulsive disorders, substance abuse or dependence, somatization disorders, antisocial personality disorders, schizophrenia, phobia, and severe cognitive impairments (Blazer & George, 1995; Myers et al., 1984). However, there was little significant difference between those age 45 to 64 and those over 65, except for severe cognitive impairment, which was higher among those over 65.

8. True. Cognitive impairment is the primary mental health problem of older age. The NIMH studies found that about 14% of the elderly had mild cognitive impairment, and about 4% had severe cases (U.S. Senate Special Committee on Aging, 1985).

9. True. Alzheimer's disease, or progressive senile dementia, is the most common cause of chronic cognitive impairment in old age (Reisberg, 1995). The essential features of this disorder are the insidious (slow) onset of dementia and a progressive deteriorating course. Multi-infarct dementia, caused by a series of strokes in the brain, is the second most common cause of cognitive impairment in old age.

10. True. By definition, there is no cure for Alzheimer's disease because it is progressive senile dementia. If the dementia is cured, then it was not Alzheimer's disease.

11. False. There is great variation in the symptoms that patients with Alzheimer's disease exhibit. Some have obviously deteriorating memory and thinking, whereas others are skillful at hiding these impairments. Some wander during the day and others wander only at night, but the majority do not wander at all. Many lose things, and others hide things but cannot remember where they hid them. A few occasionally expose themselves in public, but most do not. Some repeat the same question or action over and over; most do not. Some complain or insult their caretakers, some can be demanding, and others behave reasonably. The only things all Alzheimer's patients have in common are their confusion and impaired memory (Mace & Rabins, 1991).

12. False. The symptoms of organic brain impairment are difficult to distinguish from those of functional impairment (such as the affective or anxiety disorders) because of ambiguous diagnostic criteria, inadequate assessment techniques, and other diseases that often mask or mimic mental symptoms (Reisberg, 1995). Although accurate diagnosis is difficult, it is crucial, because recovery from reversible illness may depend on prompt and appropriate treatment.

13. False. It is best to look directly at the patient, both to establish eye contact and to see if the patient is paying attention to you (Mace & Rabins, 1991).

14. False. Talking and listening are two of the more pleasurable activities that the patient can share with others. It does not matter much what is talked about, so long as both enjoy the interaction (Mace & Rabins, 1991).

15. False. Talking about their past is usually enjoyed by older patients. This can be encouraged by showing the patient an old photograph album or some other item that may trigger memories of the past (Mace & Rabins, 1991).

16. True. The prevalence of severe cognitive impairment increases from less than 1% for persons under age 45 to about 4% for those over 65; mild cognitive impairment increases from 2% among those under 45 to about 14% among those over 65 (Myers et al., 1984).

17. True. Paranoid disorders, which are delusions of persecution or grandiosity, tend to occur in old age under adverse conditions, such as imprisonment, institutionalization, isolation, disfigurement, infections, drunkenness, or blindness. Isolation and hearing loss that results in misinterpretation of words and sounds are the primary causes (Butler & Lewis, 1982).

18. True. Poor nutrition may produce depression, confusion, apathy, and other mental symptoms (Whanger, 1980). This can become a vicious cycle, with poor nutrition causing mental symptoms that, in turn, cause even worse nutrition.

19. True. Community studies have consistently found that mental illness among the elderly is substantially more prevalent among those from the lower socioeconomic levels, regardless of whether this is measured by income, education, or former occupation (George, 1995). This is due both to the stressful effects of poverty and to the drift of mentally ill persons downward toward the lower socioeconomic levels.

20. True. About three fourths of residents of nursing homes have dementia alone or in combination with other mental disorders. Other frequent disorders are depression, anxiety, and withdrawal (Mitty, 1995).

21. False. The elderly tend to have more sleep problems than younger persons (Woodruff-Pak, 1995). Older people require longer to fall asleep, deep sleep (stage 4) virtually disappears, and there are more frequent awakenings. These problems tend to be severer among those with mental illnesses, such as severe depression or anxiety.

22. False. Major depression is less prevalent among the elderly than among younger persons. The recent NIMH surveys of four communities found that major depressive disorders (not counting bereavement) were less than half as prevalent among those over age 65 as in the general population (Blazer & George, 1995). Bereavement was more common in the oldest age group among women but not among men.

23. False. Several studies have found that widowhood is less stressful for older than for younger women (Lopata, 1995). There are several reasons for this: widowhood is not as stressful if it occurs at an expected time of life; younger widows usually face more problems, such as childbearing, returning to work, and seeking another marriage partner; and older widows can find more peers who are widowed to provide support and friendship

24. False. The aged use mental health facilities at a much lower rate than younger persons (Butler, 1995). This is partly because the aged have lower rates of mental illness in general and partly because the current generation of older people is more resistant to admitting to their mental illness and seeking treatment for it.

25. False. Psychotherapy is often effective with older patients. There is no convincing evidence that old people do poorly as psychotherapy clients (Lakin, 1995). However, there is widespread agreement that psychotherapy with older patients should be more focused and specific, more present oriented, and should use a more active therapist role.

4

How to Use the Quizzes

USING THE QUIZZES TO EDUCATE

The simplest and most common use of the FAQs and the FAMHQ is to stimulate discussion and clarify misconceptions about aging. For this purpose, I recommend using the true/false versions because they are simpler and easier to answer.

The instructor should reassure the class or workshop participants that they will not be graded on the quiz and that it is only for their own information, to be used as they see fit. They should be encouraged to answer as best as they can so they can find out what their misconceptions are. Give them about 5 minutes to answer the quiz. Encourage them to work rapidly, putting down a "?" when they do not know the answer rather than spending time puzzling over any one item.

After the students (or most of them) have finished answering the quiz, tell them that you will give them a self-scoring key to the correct answers so that they can immediately find out which they got correct and which they did not. Then either give them the key orally or post it on a blackboard or similar place where all can see.

After participants have scored their quiz, the instructor can tell them that the average person with no special education in gerontology gets about half correct, so if they got more than half correct they can feel they are "above average." If the instructor wishes she or he can ask for a show of hands for how many got "more than half right," then "more than 15 right," and then "more than 20 right" (there will be few of these). This rewards the ones who did well without embarrassing those who did not do so well.

The discussion can proceed in any of several ways, and the group can be asked which way they would like to proceed. Individuals can question or ask for discussion on those items they were most surprised about or cannot believe. Alternatively, the instructor can proceed to give the documentation for all items and discuss them in the order in which they occur in the quiz. Or the instructor may want to group for discussion those items dealing with physical aging, psychological aging, social and economic aspects, and so forth. (The items in the FAMHQ can be grouped by those dealing with frequency of mental illness in old age; those dealing with treatment of mental illness; and those with Alzheimer's disease or dementia, suicide, and so on.)

A similar use of the quizzes is to identify frequent misconceptions and areas of special interest, as an aid in planning the presentation of educational materials. This can be done by a show of hands of those who got each item correct, noting those on which there were few hands; or it can be done by asking the students to turn in their quizzes so that the frequent misconceptions can be tabulated. When the most frequent misconceptions are identified, the presentations can be organized around those topics, or the instructor can at least be sure to cover those topics in the instruction.

All who have used the quizzes to identify misconceptions and stimulate discussion report that it does succeed in stimulating much discussion. Often there is considerable argument about the validity or wording of some of the items. It is hoped that the present revisions will reduce such arguments, but some will inevitably find it difficult to accept the fact that they have misconceptions about aging. It is recommended that the instructor not enter any extended debate on the facts involved, but simply point out that the statistics and research reports speak for themselves, and if the students wish to pursue the matter further, they can look up the references and see if that satisfies them. The instructor can also recognize that there are always exceptions to general tendencies and that some people do not fit the general facts presented.

In fact, it is a good educational technique to discuss exceptions to general rules to understand why these persons are exceptions. This reinforces learning about the general rule and introduces the factors involved in the exceptions.

USING THE QUIZZES TO MEASURE LEARNING

If one wishes to measure the effects of instruction, one needs to be more careful about administration and scoring of the quizzes because any errors in scoring the pretest or posttest reduces the accuracy of the measured change. For this purpose, I recommend using the multiple-choice versions because they reduce the effect of guessing the correct answer, and, therefore, are more accurate and reliable measures of knowledge. I also recommend that the students not be allowed to score their own quizzes, first because of the temptation to change or fill in correct answers to increase the number of items correct, and, second, because of the simple mechanical and other kinds of errors that an inexperienced scorer is likely to make. Therefore, quizzes should be collected for scoring by the instructor prior to giving the correct answers.

There are two ways of measuring the effects of instruction: (1) repeat the same quiz at the beginning and end of the instruction or (2) use FAQ1 at the beginning and FAQ2 at the end of the instruction (or vice versa). The advantage of the first method is that pretest and posttest differences cannot be due to differences between the two forms. The big disadvantage is that improvements in scores may be due more to remembering the correct answers from the first administration ("practice effects") than to any increase in general knowledge about aging. The disadvantage of the second method is that differences between scores on the two forms may be due to differences in the content or wording rather than to an increase in knowledge about aging.

On balance, I recommend the use of different forms at the beginning and end because of the almost inevitable increase in scores that results from retaking the same test. This is known as the "practice effect" and cannot be avoided in test-retest situations with the same test. Although unreliability of the tests is more of a problem when using the two different forms, we have found that this tends to cancel out in the group mean scores when large groups are used. Thus, some individuals will have higher or lower scores on the second test because of chance factors (unreliability), but the group mean scores will tend to be more reliable and meaningful.

The average correlation of the FAQ1 with FAQ2 (true/false versions) in initial tests of the quizzes found an average correlation of .50 (with groups equally weighted) and higher correlations (.70 to .80) among those who knew more about aging, such as graduate students and staff at the Center on Aging and Human Development (Palmore, 1981a). These are adequate levels of between-test reliability for use of the two forms as interchangeable tests. Furthermore, Courtenay and Weidemann (1985) found that use of a "don't know" (DK) response option improved internal reliability scores dramatically. Therefore, the between-test reliability using a DK response option is probably substantially higher than the preceding correlations would indicate, as they were obtained in testing situations that did not offer this option.

The correlations between the two multiple-choice versions of the tests have not yet been tested as of this writing (1997), but they probably are higher because they are more reliable.

Finally, it is important to provide a DK response when comparing scores on the FAQ1 and FAQ2 because the DK response tends to reduce or eliminate differences in mean scores between the two quizzes (Courtenay & Weidemann, 1985). Otherwise, FAQ1 scores (true/false version) tend to be about 5% higher than those on FAQ2 (Palmore, 1981a).

USING THE QUIZZES TO TEST GROUP KNOWLEDGE

The purpose of this usage is to measure and compare levels of knowledge and most frequent misconceptions in different groups. Such comparisons are useful for understanding the causes of ignorance and prejudice toward the aged in our society. These comparisons are also useful for determining which groups are most in need of information to correct their misconceptions about aging. Fortunately, enough groups have been studied so that we have some standards against which any new groups tested can be compared (see Chapter 5 and the abstracts).

This usage is similar in method to the measurement of the effects of instruction because it is important to get accurate scoring. Therefore, I recommend the multiple-choice versions for this purpose and recommend that the respondents not score their own quizzes. Also it is important that respondents be given plenty of time to finish answering because rushing can artificially lower scores.

A feature of the revised forms used in this handbook is that there is a DK response allowed. This permits a distinction between misconceptions (wrong answers) and ignorance (DK answers), a theoretically and practically important distinction. A misconception involves a belief that one knows the correct answer when actually one does not. Ignorance involves a recognition that one does not know the correct answer. In other words, a misconception is a wrong idea, whereas ignorance is an absence of an idea. It is usually more difficult to correct a misconception than to change ignorance into knowledge. In a sense, correcting a misconception involves two steps: One must first become convinced that one was wrong and then must be convinced that the right answer is indeed correct.

Thus, on the revised tests, there are three different scores that may be used to measure levels of knowledge: the percentage correct, the percentage wrong, and the percentage of DK responses. Each of these scores measures different things and is useful for different purposes. The percentage correct measures the overall amount of knowledge. The percentage wrong measures the amount of misconception that needs to be corrected. The percentage of DK responses measures the amount of ignorance that needs information.

USING THE QUIZZES TO MEASURE ATTITUDES

The percentage-wrong measure just discussed is the basis for measuring attitudes; however, it should be noted that the FAQs are not the best way of measuring attitudes (see Chapter 5). However, the better ones, such as Rosencranz and McNevin (1969), are lengthy and time-consuming. If one is limited in the amount of time or cooperation one can get from subjects, one can use the bias scores from the FAQ1, FAQ2, or FAMHQ, as indirect measures of attitudes toward the aged. The bias scores are based on the assumption that certain misconceptions about the aged indicate positive or negative bias. For example, if someone thinks it is true that a majority of old people are senile, it probably indicates a negative bias toward the aged. Conversely, if someone denies that the five senses tend to decline in old age, it probably indicates a positive bias toward the aged.

We have classified 16 items of the true/false version of the FAQ1 as indicating a negative bias if they are marked incorrectly: Items 1, 3, 5, 7 to 11, 13, 16 to 18, 21, 22, 24, and 25. Conversely, we have classified 5 items as indicating a positive bias if they are marked incorrectly: 2, 4, 6, 12, and 14.

In the true/false version of the FAQ2 the negative-bias items are 3, 4, 5, 9 to 11, 12, 14, 17, 19 to 21, 24, and 25. The five FAQ2 positive-bias items are 1, 2, 8, 13, and 16.

Using these items, one can compute three measures of bias: an anti-aged bias score, a pro-aged bias score, and a net bias score. The anti-aged bias score is the percentage of the negative-bias items marked wrong (number wrong divided by number of possible negative-bias items).

The pro-aged bias score is the percentage of the positive-bias items marked wrong. The net bias score is the pro-aged score (% positive errors) minus the anti-aged score (% negative errors). If the resulting score is negative, it indicates a net anti-aged bias; if it is positive, it indicates a net pro-aged bias. For practical purposes, any individual net bias score in the range of ± 20% (the difference made by each pro-aged item) is probably not significantly different from zero and should be considered a neutral bias score. However, such scores should be included in the computation of the group's mean score. Note that one does not count DK responses as incorrect for these purposes because simple ignorance about a fact does not usually indicate a biased attitude. Also note that subtracting percentages of errors (rather than raw numbers) to compute the net bias score controls for the fact that there are more negative- than positive-bias items. The net bias score simply shows the tendency of the person (or group) to think positively or negatively about the elderly.

When using the multiple-choice versions, the computation is slightly different. To compute the anti-aged bias score, one divides the number of negative bias options marked, by the total number of items in the quiz with a negative option. In the FAQ1, there are 18 items with a negative bias option; in the FAQ2, there are 16 such items; and the FAMHQ also has 14 such items.

Similarly, to compute the pro-aged bias score, one divides the number of positive bias options marked, by the total number of items in the quiz with a positive-bias option. In the FAQ1, there are 13 such items; in the FAQ2 there are 8 such items; and in the FAMHQ, there are 12 such items.

Then to compute the net bias score one proceeds the same way as in the true/false versions: subtract the anti-aged bias score from the pro-aged bias score.

CREATING THE PSYCHOLOGICAL FACTS ON AGING QUIZ

McCutcheon (1986) proposed a combination of items from the FAQ1 and the FAQ2 with two original items to form a quiz dealing exclusively with psychological and sociological facts about aging. She proposed combining items 1, 2, 3, 5, 11, 12, 15, 20, 23, and 24 from the FAQ1 with Items 5, 12 to 14, 16, 17, 19, 20, 23, and 24 from the FAQ2, and the following two original items:

1. Well over 90% of all grandparents greatly enjoy being grandparents. (False)
2. Older people tend to become more concerned with their health or bodily functions as they grow older. (True)

The documentation for the first original item comes from Lopata (1973) and Neugarten and Weinstein (1964), who show that only about half of all grandparents greatly enjoy that role. The documentation for the second original item comes from Earley and von Mering (1969) and Neugarten and Gutmann (1964),whose studies show that people do become more concerned about their health as they grow older. (*Note:* This item has been reworded to avoid the phrase "preoccupied with their health," which was in the first version, because "preoccupation" is difficult to define and measure.)

When the resulting Psychological Facts on Aging Quiz (PFAQ) was administered to 121 subjects in introductory psychology classes, the mean score correct was 60% (McCutcheon, 1986), which is similar to the scores of college students on the FAQ1 and FAQ2, without the DK option. The scores were also not significantly different by gender or age, which is also similar to the results on the FAQ1 and FAQ2 (see Chapter 5). The PFAQ appears to be a useful variation for those who want to focus on these aspects of aging, either in instruction or in measurement. However, one could make a much longer "social-psychological" facts on aging quiz by adding the following items that also have psychological, social, or economic relevance: from FAQ1, items 7, 8, 9, 13, 14, 16 to 18, 21, and 22; from FAQ2, Items 8 to 10, 11, 15, 18, 21, and 25.

SUMMARY

There are four main uses for the FAQs, and the method of administration is somewhat different depending on the purpose. The quizzes can be true/false and self-scored when the primary purpose is educational, but for the other uses, it is best to use multiple choice and to have a non-respondent do the scoring because of the errors that are likely with self-scoring. A Psychological Facts on Aging Quiz contains items from FAQ 1, FAQ2, and two original items, all of which deal with psychological or social aspects of aging.

The true/false versions are recommended for the purpose of stimulating discussion and correction of misconceptions because it is easier and quicker to take and to score. The multiple-choice versions are recommended for testing knowledge and measuring learning.

5

Results of Studies Using the Quizzes

The detailed results of 150 studies using the FAQs are presented in Part II, but we will summarize their main findings and trends in this chapter.

OVERALL KNOWLEDGE

The overall and most disturbing general finding is that most people know little about aging and have many misconceptions. The average person (those with high school or less education) tends to get a little better than half the items correct on all the quizzes. Because one would be expected to get half the items correct just by chance alone (in a true/false format), it appears that the average person knows almost nothing about aging. Or, to put it differently, the average person appears to have almost as many misconceptions about aging as correct conceptions.

Graduate students and professionals dealing with the aged usually missed about a third of the true/false items. Even gerontology students and faculty in various studies missed from one tenth to one third of the items.

A similar finding emerges from the use of the multiple-choice format. On the FAQ1 multiple choice, the mean correct answers among college sociology students was 41%; on the FAQ2, the mean correct answers was 44% (Harris & Changes, 1994; Harris, Changes, & Palmore, 1996).

This means that the students either had misconceptions or were ignorant about the facts on the majority of items.

The implications of this general finding for gerontology and education in general seem clear: We have not been adequately educating our students and the public about aging, a most basic process that affects every individual and group.

KNOWLEDGE LEVELS AND EDUCATION

The main variable that makes a significant and fairly consistent difference in overall levels of knowledge, is education.

Those with high school (or less) education had scores of about 52% to 60%; the college or technical school groups had scores of 55% to 69%; the graduate school groups had scores of 65% to 76%; and the gerontology students and faculty had scores of 66% to 92%. Most significantly, those groups who have studied gerontology get most of the answers correct. Faculty of the Duke Center on Aging got 90% correct (Palmore, 1977), dental students after a geriatrics course got 94% (Broder & Block, 1986), and graduate students in gerontology got 92% (McKinlay, 1979a).

Furthermore, most of the studies that compared differences in knowledge between educational levels within their studies also found that the more educated had higher mean scores on the FAQ1. For example, this was true among radiographers (Dowd, 1983), medical students (Holtzman & Beck, 1981), undergraduate and graduate students (Jeffrey, 1979), Australian undergraduates (Luszcz, 1982), nurses (McDowell, 1978), nursing students (Williams, 1982), undergraduate students in gerontology and in nongerontology courses (Kline & Kline, 1991a), and the aged themselves (McKinley, 1979b).

This tendency is probably due to two main factors: increased general knowledge and increased test sophistication. As educational levels increase, general knowledge, which apparently includes some knowledge about aging, increases. Second, as educational levels increase, so does test sophistication or skill at taking tests, which includes the ability to guess correct answers when one is not sure of the answer. These factors are reflected in the higher scores.

KNOWLEDGE AND OTHER VARIABLES

Knowledge levels (as measured by the FAQ1) do not seem to vary significantly or consistently between the sexes, between age groups, between sections of the country, between Blacks and Whites, between occupational groups, between persons with low or high contact with elders, or with regard to any other grouping that has been studied so far, once educational levels are controlled. For example, Barnet (1979) found no significant differences between various occupational groups who were staff members of a community mental health center; West and Levy (1984) found no significant differences between medical specialties; and Kabacoff, Shaw, Putnam, and Nein (1983) found no significant difference between administrators and service workers in agencies dealing with the elderly. Studies of physicians (Coe, Miller, Prendergast, & Grossberg, 1982; Levy & West, 1985), medical and dental students (Holtzman & Beck, 1979, 1981), occupational therapists (Bressler, 1996), clergy (Levy & West, 1985; Wallace & Wallace, 1982), social workers (Levy & West, 1985), nurses (Walter, 1986; Wexler, 1979), and undergraduates (Palmore, 1980) all find average FAQ1 scores of between 65% and 70%.

This is a rather surprising set of negative findings because one might think that older persons would know more about aging, or that perhaps women might be more sensitive or concerned about the problems of aging for various reasons, or that people in some occupations dealing extensively with the aged might know more about aging; however, apparently none of these assumptions is true. Older people tend to be just as ignorant about aging and have about as many misconceptions and stereotypes about themselves as do younger persons. Apparently one does not learn facts about aging automatically as one ages. One must have formal educational experiences to learn these facts. Conversely, we know from several studies that these facts can be learned in classes and workshops because the scores do increase after these experiences (see later sections of this chapter, on changes in knowledge and bias).

One policy implication of this "negative" finding is the need to provide more information about aging to all types of persons, old and young, men and women, Black and White, service occupations and nonservice occupations, and so forth.

Similarly, most of the studies of contact with older persons and knowledge about aging find little or no effects of contact on knowledge (Allen, 1981; Knox, Gekoski, & Johnson, 1986; Koyan, Inoue, & Shibata, 1987; Miller & Dodder, 1984; Perotta, Perkins, Schimpfhauser, & Calkins, 1981). Only Barnet (1979) found a small association ($r = .18$) between knowledge and contact with elderly among the staff of a community mental health center. This may have been due to the greater education of those who had more contact with the elderly. Rabins and Motts (1981) found that nonphysician staff members of a psychiatric unit had a significant increase (11 points) in FAQ1 scores after the unit became a psychogeriatric unit. They attributed this increase to the increased contact with the elderly through patient care and teaching conferences. But the increase could have been mainly the result of teaching conferences and other learning experiences not directly related to contact with the elderly.

Thus, the widespread assumption that simple contact with the elderly will increase knowledge about the aged also appears to be false. We shall see that contact can affect attitudes toward the aged (see later section on "Bias and Other Variables"), but the studies just cited indicate that it does not usually affect general knowledge about aging. Apparently, contact with the aged is usually limited to a few persons who often are not typical of the average aged person, so generalizations from these few to the total aged population tend to be inaccurate.

One study of the relationship between knowledge of aging and attitudes toward programs for the aged did find a few significant associations. Brubaker and Barresi (1979) found that social workers' knowledge about aging was higher among those who believed government services to the elderly should not be viewed as unique for the aged. However, level of knowledge generally made little or no difference in attitudes toward service delivery. Similarly, Klemmack and Roff (1981) found no significant correlations between FAQ1 scores and attitudes toward government support for the elderly. Apparently, knowing more about the aged does not usually lead to different attitudes toward programs for the aged. These attitudes are probably based more on general attitudes toward government programs and social services.

FREQUENT MISCONCEPTIONS

The studies that reported the most frequent misconceptions (items on which the majority did not have correct answers) tended to find a common set of misconceptions. In the FAQ1 this set included the beliefs that at least one tenth of the aged live in long-stay institutions (Item 7); that the majority are usually unable to adapt to change (Item 11); that the majority are often bored (Item 16); that over 15% of the population is over age 65 (Item 19); that the majority have incomes below the poverty line (Item 21); that old people tend to become more religious as they age (Item 23); and that the majority are often irritated or angry (Item 24). In the FAQ2 the most frequent misconceptions include the beliefs that older persons have more injuries in the home than younger persons (Item 4); that life expectancy for Whites at age 65 is greater than for Blacks (Item 6); that Social Security benefits do not automatically increase with inflation (Item 9); that SSI does not guarantee a minimum income for needy aged (Item 10); that the aged do not get their proportionate share of the nation's income (Item 11); that the aged have higher rates of criminal victimization (Item 12); that there are about equal numbers of widows and widowers among the aged (Item 15); that the majority live alone (Item 20); and that the majority of parents have serious problems adjusting to their "empty nest" (Item 24).

In the FAMHQ the most frequent misconceptions (listed in order of frequency) include the belief that the majority of nursing home patients do not suffer from mental illness (Item 20); that the aged do not have fewer mental impairments than do younger persons (Item 7); that mental illness is not more common among the elderly in lower socioeconomic groups (Item 19); and that widowhood is not more stressful for younger women (Item 23).

Note that most of these frequent misconceptions represent negative stereotypes about the aged. In the FAQ1, five of the seven frequent misconceptions are clearly negative stereotypes, and another one (Item 19) exaggerates the problem of the aged by exaggerating the number of aged. In the FAQ2, seven of the nine frequent misconceptions represent negative stereotypes. This tendency of the frequent misconceptions to represent negative stereotypes, rather than positive or neutral images of the aged, supports the general finding that the average person tends to have a negative net bias score. We will discuss this further in the next section.

KNOWLEDGE AND BIAS TOWARD AGING

There is considerable and fairly consistent evidence that knowledge about aging has a modest but significant correlation with attitudes toward aging; that is, those with more knowledge tend to have less negative and more positive attitudes. Faculty in gerontology, who have high knowledge about aging, have low anti-aged bias scores (11) and almost neutral net bias scores (–2) (Palmore, 1977). Similarly, college students have both higher FAQ1 scores and lower net bias scores than high school students (Allen, 1981). Third-year medical students who have had a course on geriatrics have higher FAQ1 scores and an almost neutral net bias score (+2), compared with other medical and dental students, who have net bias scores of from –8 to –15 (Holtzman & Beck, 1981). Linn & Zeppa (1987) found greater knowledge as measured by the FAQ2 predicted more positive attitudes toward the elderly among medical students.

The total FAQ scores tend to have significant negative correlations with anti-aged bias (Auserman, 1991; Dodson, 1990; Durand & Klemmack, 1981; Jones, 1993; Klemmack, 1978; Patwell, 1991). In fact, this led Klemmack to conclude that the FAQ1 is more a measure of attitude than of knowledge (see Palmore, 1978, for a rebuttal to this conclusion). Miller and Dodder (1984) found that the anti-aged bias score correlated negatively with most of their 13 measures of "knowledge" about the aged (actually measures of contact, social distance, and education in gerontology), and that three of these were significant correlations. Most of the studies examining the relationship of FAQ1 scores and measures of attitudes from other scales have found modest ($r = .17$ to $.27$) but significant relationships (Harris, 1979; Holtzman & Beck, 1979; Iannone, 1986; Monk & Kaye, 1982; Steinhauer & Brockway, 1980). Only Ellor and Altfeld (1980) found no significant correlation between the FAQ1 score and their own attitude-toward-aging scale. This negative result may be due to a lack of validity or reliability of their attitude scale.

BIAS AND OTHER VARIABLES

There is considerable evidence from FAQ1 studies that there are differences among occupational groups in their biases, but most of these studies need to be replicated before we can be confident of their general validity. Levy and West (1985, 1989) found that clergy had the highest positive net bias score (+13) of the three professions they studied; social workers had a net bias of almost as high (+10), although social workers in aging had a slightly negative net bias (–4); and physicians had an almost neutral net bias score (–2). West and Levy (1984) also found that physicians in internal medicine tended to have neutral bias scores, whereas other specialties tended to have negative bias scores. A similar difference was found by Belgrave, Lavin, Breslau, and Haug (1982): There were more negative stereotypes among medical students intending to specialize in surgery than among those intending to specialize in family practice or internal medicine.

Walter (1986) found that nurses in long-term care institutions had an average net bias score of –12. Keller (1986) as well as Williams (1982) also found that nurses in long-term care institutions had more negative net bias scores than other nurses. This may be due to nurses in long-term care institutions having greater exposure to more aged people who fit the negative stereotypes.

Keller (1986) found a rather large negative net bias score (–25) for the average health professional in North Carolina. In contrast, McDowell (1978) found a positive net bias score (+20) among North Carolina nurses in ambulatory and home care.

More recently, Ausherman (1991) found that junior high school health teachers' knowledge was moderately low, and their attitudes were slightly positive.

Although contact with the elderly does not usually seem to increase knowledge, it does appear to increase positive attitudes and decrease negative attitudes. Miller and Dodder (1984) found that the pro-aged bias scores increased significantly with increases in their total contact measure and most of its subscales. Similarly, the anti-aged bias scores tended to decrease with more contact. This is in contrast, however, to the studies of nurses mentioned earlier, which showed that more contact with elderly in nursing homes seemed to increase negative bias. Carmel et al. (1990) found that work experience with elderly patients did have a positive effect, especially among family physicians, on the willingness of physicians to continue to work with the elderly.

Thus, the type of elderly person contacted appears to affect whether attitudes will become more positive or negative. In terms of gender and age, West and Levy (1981) found elderly men and the old-old to have greater anti-aged bias than elderly females and the young-old. Perhaps elderly men tend to be more negative than elderly women about things in general, and the old-old are more negative about aging because they experience directly more of its negative aspects. However, these findings need to be replicated before assuming their general validity.

There have been some associations found between attitudes toward the aged and other attitudes. For example, Eakes (1986) found that anti-aged bias correlated significantly (r = 21) with death anxiety: Those more anxious about death tended to be more biased against aging. Kahana and Kiyak (1984) found that staff members in nursing homes who were more biased, either pro-aging or anti-aging, tended to encourage more dependence among their patients. Also, those who were more pro-aged biased were less likely to exhibit positive parenting and positive affection toward their patients.

Miller and Acuff (1982) found that those with more pro-aged bias had poorer health, and those with more anti-aged bias wanted to work more and had more income. Explanations for these relationships are not obvious, and the study needs replication.

Groseck (1989) found that both knowledge and attitudes toward elders were positively related to life satisfaction among a random sample of Philadelphians. Conversely, Mishaan (1992) found no significant relationship between knowledge (FAQ1) and life satisfaction among a group of Brooklyn aged persons. It is unclear whether there is any causal relationship here, or if so, in which direction the causality runs.

CHANGES IN KNOWLEDGE

One of the most frequent uses of the FAQs is to measure change in knowledge before and after some educational experience on aging. There have been over two dozen studies of change in knowledge using the FAQ1 reported so far. Of these, only six failed to find a significant increase in knowledge after some educational experience on aging. Each of these exceptions is understandable, given the unusual nature of the "educational experience."

Chandler et al. (1986) found no significant effect of an "experiential education program" about aging. Apparently there was little factual content.

Doka (1986) failed to find a significant effect on FAQ1 scores of an oral history project for adolescents. Apparently, simply getting to know an older person through interviews does not increase knowledge about aging in general. Similarly, Greenhill and Baker (1986) failed to find a significant increase in knowledge about aging among a group of nursing students who had a planned experience getting to know older adults well in comparison with a control group of nurses without that experience.

Patwell (1991) found no significant gains in knowledge (nor in attitudes) after a yearlong "aging awareness" program. Satterfield, Yasumara, and Goodman (1984) found no significant increase in the FAQ1 scores among the elderly after a physical therapy course that included attempts to correct misconceptions.

Note that none of these experiences included classroom didactic experiences. West and Ernst (1981) found a small but statistically insignificant increase after a life-enrichment program for 18 older adults. If there had been a larger group, this increase would probably be significant. All the other studies found significant increases, although some did not have a control or comparison group. I will briefly describe the major studies here in alphabetical order.

Blackwell (1979) found significant increases in five (1, 2, 4, 11, and 20) out of seven items from the FAQ1, administered to workers with the aged after a workshop on aging. Broder and Block (1986) found an increase of 26% (from 62% to 94%) after a geriatric course for dental students. However, they also found that after 1 to 2 years their mean scores declined to 76%, showing an 18% loss of knowledge over time. Burris (1992) found that nurses who had a seminar about aging had an average score of 78% correct compared with a score of 58% correct for those in a control group.

Byrd (1984) found an increase of 44% (from 52% to 96%) after a course in peer counseling for older adults. This is the largest increase on record and probably reflects extensive discussion of the correct answers before the posttest.

Carmel et al. (1992) found that courses in gerontology and geriatrics among medical, nursing, and social work students in Israel increased the nurses' scores by 8% and the social work students' by 12%; however, no increase occurred among medical students. Dail and Johnson (1985) found an increase of 8% after a 5-week section on aging in an undergraduate course in human development. Donnelly, Duthie, Kirsling, and Gambert (1985) found a modest but significant increase of 6% among medical students over 3 years of their medical training.

Duthie and Gambert (1983) found significant improvement in knowledge about psychiatric and biomedical items in the FAQ1 among internal medicine residents after a geriatric medicine rotation. There was no improvement, however, on the social items. Apparently these residents were not taught anything about social gerontology. Greenslade (1986) found a 22% increase in FAQ1 scores among nurses after a postgraduate geriatric nursing program, whereas there was no significant change among a control group. Hannon (1980) also found an increase (from 68% to 78%) among graduate nurses after a course on aging. King and Cobb (1983) found reductions in errors among nursing students on 17 of the 24 items in the FAQ1 following an 11-week rotation with the aged; however, the change in mean scores (4%) was not tested for statistical significance.

Laner (1981) reported two studies with significant increases in the FAQ1 scores. In the first study the quiz was given before a social gerontology course, and the answers were freely discussed. After this discussion and the end of the course, the scores increased by 20%. The study was repeated but without the discussion of the correct answers. Again, the scores increased significantly after the course, although there was less of an increase (13%).

Levenson (1978) found a modest but significant increase of 7% after a course in psychology with emphasis on human development. Linsk and Pinkston (1984) also found a small but significant increase (5%) in FAQ1 scores among human service practitioners specializing in the elderly, after a 15-hour course designed to improve their care of the elderly. Okuma and Johnson (1986) found that elementary school children had a 23% improvement in FAQ1 scores after a unit on aging. Riddick (1985) found an increase of 20% among geriatric recreation service providers after an educational program on aging.

There was no change in a control group. Ross (1983) found an increase of 14% among nursing students after a planned learning experience with well elderly. Shenk and Lee (1995) found improvements in knowledge (FAQ1) among professional service providers after a continuing education course on gerontology.

Smith (1985) found an increase of 12% among physical therapy students over the 2 years of their training. Smith et al (1989) found an increase in knowledge among Mississippi pharmacists of 16% after a geriatric education course. Steinhauer and Brockway (1980) found public management students had a significant increase in knowledge after a gerontology course, whereas there was no change in a control group. Wilson and Glamser (1982) found a small increase of 496 among osteopathic medical students after a unit on aging. This was not tested for statistical significance. Zigarmi (1986) found a small but significant increase of 8% after a unit on aging among middle school students.

Ansello and Lamy (1987) tested pharmacists using FAQ1 before and after training in geropharmacy and gerontology in three formats: weekly, weekend, and monthly. The weekly and weekend formats produced more knowledge gains than the monthly format. The mean percentage point gain was 9%.

More recently, a study of the effects of a geriatric course on knowledge among optometry students (Anonymous, 1992) found scores on the FAQ1 increased significantly after the course in two classes in which the geriatric course was combined with a geriatric clinic.

Thus, most of the studies using the FAQ1 to measure learning about aging found significant (although often small) increases in scores after the educational experience. Of special note is the wide variety of settings and types of students involved.

CHANGES IN ATTITUDES

Several of the preceding studies also used the bias scores in the FAQ1 to test whether or not there was any change in attitudes toward the aged. In contrast to the generally positive results in learning, the change in attitudes with the FAQ1 was negative.

Doka (1986) found no change in the bias scores among adolescents after an oral history project dealing with older people. This is consistent with the lack of any increase in knowledge scores. Hannon (1980) also found no change in the FAQ1 bias scores among graduate nurses after a course on aging. However, the Kogan Attitudes Toward Old People

Scale (Kogan, 1961) was also administered before and after the course, and it showed a significant change toward more favorable attitudes. This indicates that the Kogan Scale is a more sensitive measure of attitudes than are the FAQ1 bias scores.

King and Cobb (1983) found a small decrease in the net bias score (from −8 to −6), but this was probably not statistically significant. Levenson (1978) found a small decrease in anti-aged bias scores among undergraduates after a course in psychology, but this decrease was not statistically significant. It is noteworthy that Levenson found a small but significant increase in knowledge after this course. Ross (1983) found no significant change in the net bias scores among nursing students after a learning experience with well elderly; however, this study did find a significant increase in knowledge. Smith (1985) found no consistent pattern of change in bias scores among physical therapy students over the 2 years of their training.

I conclude from these studies that the FAQ1 is not a useful and sensitive way of measuring change in attitudes toward the aged. Several other studies (Murphy, Die, & Walker, 1986; Steinhauer & Brockway, 1980; Wilson & Glamser, 1982; Zigarmi, 1986) have found significant changes in attitudes using other measures of attitudes such as the Kogan Scale or the Rosencranz and McNevin Semantic Differential Scale. These scales, therefore, appear to be better methods of measuring change in attitudes toward the aged.

INTERNATIONAL COMPARISONS

Although the FAQ1 was designed to be used in the United States, it has been used by several investigators in four other countries: Australia, Britain, Canada, and Japan. In each such study the wording was modified to make it appropriate to the given country. In Japan it was, of course, translated into Japanese. One of the versions used in Canada was translated into French (Goulet, 1982).

In Australia, Luszcz (1982) and Luszcz and Fitzgerald (1986) did two interesting studies. The first was a study of first- and third-year college undergraduates. This study found that the mean percentages of correct answers (58% among first-year and 64% among third-year students) were similar to scores on the FAQ1 among U.S. college students.

Also, the most frequent misconceptions were similar to those in the United States (Items 7, 11, 18–21, and 24). The net bias scores (–17 and –19) were higher than those of U.S. college students reported by Palmore (1977).

The second study (Luszcz & Fitzgerald, 1986) compared three generations: adolescents, middle-aged people, and elders. The adolescents had lower (60%) FAQ1 scores than did middle-aged (67%) and aged persons (69%). This may have been due to the lower education of the adolescents, who had not yet finished high school. However, the three generations were similar to each other (and to the U.S. samples; e.g., Palmore, 1977) in terms of the items revealing the most frequent misconceptions.

In Canada there were two studies of nurses and one of social work students. Wexler (1979) found that public health nurses had a mean percentage of correct answers of 68% and that the most frequent misconceptions were Items 7, 16, 17, 19, 21, 24, and 25. These results are similar to those of studies with U.S. nurses (e.g., Hannon, 1980, and Huckstadt, 1983). Greenslade (1986) found that a group of Canadian nurses working with the elderly but with no gerontology training scored 61% correct, whereas a similar group with some postgraduate training in geriatrics scored 83% correct. Similar effects of gerontology training have been found in the United States (Hannon, 1980).

Kwan (1982) examined the adequacy of the FAQ1 as a measure of bias among social work students at the University of British Columbia. He concluded that it was not a valid instrument for this purpose. This is similar to the conclusions of several U.S. studies, as noted earlier.

Steel (1987) found that dental students in British and Irish schools had little knowledge of aging (59% correct on FAQ1) and more negative attitudes toward older people than toward the young. Physics students had more knowledge and more positive attitudes toward older people than did the dental students.

There have been four studies using the FAQ1 in Japan, all in Tokyo. The first was a cross-cultural comparison of middle-aged married persons in Tokyo and Winston-Salem, NC (Maeda, 1981; Romeis & Sussman, 1980). This study found similar percentages of correct answers in Tokyo (53%) and Winston-Salem (55%) but much more negative net bias scores in Tokyo (–39) than in Winston-Salem (–18).

This may reflect a greater negative bias among the Tokyo sample, but I suspect it probably reflects some distortion in the Japanese translation, which artificially increases the Japanese negative bias score. However, Romeis and Sussman (1980) reported that an alternative method of computing the net bias score reduced the difference between the Tokyo and Winston-Salem samples to only two points. Maeda (1981) also found that these middle-aged men tended to have higher FAQ1 scores if they were older, which is contrary to the lack of association between FAQ1 scores and age in the United States. Interestingly, he also found that women who had related negatively to their mothers in childhood tended to have more negative bias toward aging.

Another study of adults in Tokyo (Anonymous, 1986) found similar knowledge scores (57%) to those in the United States but found substantially more negative net bias scores (–38). Again I suspect this is the result of some artifact in the translation rather than a reflection of more bias against Japanese aged (Palmore, 1985).

The third Tokyo study (Sakata & Okamoto, 1985) was of caregivers in nursing homes. They found that those with higher FAQ1 scores were more educated and had more positive attitudes toward social welfare services, whereas those with more negative bias scores had higher tension or frustration scores but higher self-estimation of social status. Tojo and Maeda (1985) also reported that these caregivers with higher FAQ1 scores tended to have less negative bias but lower job satisfaction scores. This may have been because they had more education.

The fourth Japanese study found low levels of knowledge (57% correct); educational level was positively related to knowledge; and negative misconceptions about old age are commonly held by Japanese adults (Koyano, 1987).

Thus, the international studies using the FAQ1 generally show similar results to those in the United States, with the exception that the Tokyo studies find more negative bias scores than in the United States. This difference may be more an artifact of the translation (or method of scoring) than of any real difference in attitudes between Japanese and Americans.

VALIDITY AND RELIABILITY

Klemmack (1978) questions the validity of the FAQ1 as a measure of knowledge about the aged. He has three criticisms: (a) the discriminatory power of the seven items with highest or lowest scores is below the "usual standard for tests"; (b) item-to-total-score correlation coefficients are not statistically significant for 18 of the items and, of the remaining seven items, only four have the predicted positive relationships; and (c) most of the items designated as reflecting positive or negative bias show the expected loadings on the first principle factor (derived from a factor analysis), which indicates that the test is more a measure of attitude than of knowledge. Norris et al. (1987) also criticized the FAQ because they found that the factor structure derived from responses was different from those "determined intuitively" by Palmore. (See Palmore [1988], for a response to this criticism.)

The criteria used by Klemmack and by Norris et al. to question the validity of the FAQ1 are inappropriate criteria for assessing a tool whose primary purposes are to measure levels of information, identify most frequent misconceptions, and measure changes in information. Klemmack's criteria would be appropriate if the quiz were primarily "psychometric" in purpose, that is, if it were designed primarily to place a person relative to a normative group on a relatively stable and homogeneous trait (such as intelligence).

On the contrary, however, the quiz's purpose is primarily "edumetric" (Carver, 1974); that is, it was designed to yield measurements that are directly interpretable in terms of specified performance standards. The specified performance standard in this case is the ability to distinguish correctly the truth or falsity of statements about aging. Given this standard, it is irrelevant whether an item has high or low discriminatory power or has a high item-to-total-score correlation. Similarly, the fact that many of the items load heavily on a factor that could be called the "negative-positive image of aging" also has nothing to do with its validity as a fact about aging.

An analogy may clarify this point. If one wanted to test knowledge about state capitals, it would be perfectly valid to construct a quiz consisting of 25 true or false statements about which cities are capitals of which states. The discriminatory power and item-to-total-score correlations of many of the items might be low, but this would be irrelevant to the validity of those items as measures of knowledge about state capitals. Those students who got more items correct probably know more about state capitals than do other students.

Of course, successful guessing might inflate a student's score, but this is a problem with any closed-answer quiz. Similarly, the 25 states chosen for the quiz may match one student's knowledge better than another's. There may also be factors in the quiz that would appear in a factor analysis, such as those relating to region of the country or size of the state. None of these things, however, would challenge the validity of the quiz or its items.

The primary evidence for the validity of the quiz is the documentation of the items, which cites the statistics and studies demonstrating the facts. Most of the statistics or findings come from representative national studies or have been substantiated by several local studies and are generally agreed on by the experts in the area. Thus, all the items have a high degree of "face validity."

Another support for the FAQ1's validity is the fact that those who have been trained in gerontology and should know more about aging do tend to score higher on it, as discussed earlier. Group score reliability also is high, as shown by the consistency with which comparable educational groups have similar mean scores, and by similar scores on test and retest. The reliability of rank ordering of the items in terms of percentage wrong is also high, as shown by the consistency with which the most frequent misconceptions are identified by most of the studies (see abstracts).

However, as Klemmack (1978) recognizes, item-to-total-score reliability is low because several items do not correlate well with the total scores. That is, different people get different sets of items right, depending on which areas of aging they happen to know about. If the items with lowest item-to-total-score correlations were omitted, the quiz's item reliability would be improved, but then some of the most basic facts and most frequent misconceptions would be omitted. I recommend inclusion of all 25 items in order to cover the range of basic facts and frequent misconceptions.

It is encouraging that adding a DK option reduces guessing and substantially improves the quiz's reliability (Clark, 1996; Courtenay & Weidemann, 1985; Richardson, 1991). For this reason (and others), we now recommend using the DK option.

Kline et al. (1990) did an "experiment" which they claim shows that the FAQ1 is "vulnerable to bias," because there are more negative bias items (if answered wrong) than positive bias items. They told young adults to complete the FAQ under instructions to adopt either a positive or negative bias toward the elderly, or to adopt a neutral attitude in their responses. They found that scores on the FAQ were "greatly affected by the direction of the bias." They then developed a new Knowledge of Aging and the Elderly (KAE) questionnaire, which is balanced in item valence.

However, as I pointed out in my response (1990), this balancing of the number of negative and positive items is theoretically a good idea, but it does not make much difference in practice (no significant difference in mean scores). The "experiment" simply showed that college students can perceive the positive or negative valence of many of the items and can, therefore, bias their answers when told to do so. Furthermore, there are several errors and dubious assumptions in the KAE that make it a less valid test of knowledge than the FAQ. (See Kline & Kline [1991a], for another comparison of the FAQ and the KAE.)

RESULTS OF FAQ2

The FAQ2 was designed primarily to be used as an alternate form to the FAQ1 for test-retest purposes. The FAQ2 allows the measurement of learning without the problems of "practice effects" or of students remembering the correct answer to the quiz from the first administration. However, it can be used for all the same purposes as the FAQ1.

In contrast to the 90 or more studies using the FAQ1, there have been only a few studies using the FAQ2 (Clark, 1996; Courtenay & Weidemann, 1985; Dudley, 1992; Duerson et al., 1992; Linn & Zeppa, 1987; Lusk et al., 1990; Palmore, 1981a; Pulliam & Dancer, 1996; Smith et al., 1989).

The first use was our pretest of the quiz (Palmore, 1981a) with various groups of students, staff, and faculty at Duke (N = 114) and at a workshop on aging (N = 28). We found that these groups tended to get higher scores (% correct) on the first quiz than on the second. This discrepancy ranged from an average of 5 percentage points for persons untrained in gerontology (FAQ1 = 67%; FAQ2 = 62%) to a discrepancy of 26 points for persons with some training in gerontology (FAQ1 = 84%; FAQ2 = 58%). One explanation for this is that those with some training in gerontology have learned many of the facts in the first quiz but few of those in the second quiz. This is understandable because the first form has been widely used at many aging centers, so gerontology students and staff are more likely to be familiar with the facts in the first quiz.

However, Courtenay and Weidemann (1985) as well as Clark (1996) found that using a DK optional response eliminated the discrepancies between the percentages correct on the two quizzes. This suggests that people tend to guess correctly more of the answers on the FAQ1 than the FAQ2 and thus get a higher score on the FAQ1. When this guessing is reduced by giving a DK option, the proportion of items that are really known and responded to correctly is about the same in the two quizzes. Therefore, we strongly recommend providing a DK response when results from the two quizzes are to be compared.

We found in the pretests (which did not use a DK option) that the average correlation between the first and second quiz was .50, and that groups who knew more about aging had higher correlations (.70 & .80). However, Lusk et al. (1990) found almost no correlation between scores on the two quizzes ($r = .04$)—when there was no DK option. But Clark (1996) found that the two quizzes had a correlation of .68 when the DK option was used. Presumably, using the DK option reduces guessing, which increases these correlations. Dudley (1992) even found a correlation of .91 between the two quizzes when the DK option was used.

As for identifying frequent misconceptions, Courtenay and Weidemann's (1985) study using the FAQ2 (with a DK response) resulted in seven items (6, 9, 11, 12, 15, 20, and 24) on which half or more students had errors (as opposed to the simple ignorance indicated by a DK response). As shown in Table 5.1, the most frequent misconception (true/false version) was on Item 9, which 89% answered incorrectly, showing their belief that Social Security benefits do not automatically increase with inflation. This was followed by Item 24 (81% incorrect), the belief that the majority of parents have serious problems when the last child leaves home. About two thirds thought there were only two widows for each widower (Item 15), and almost two thirds thought the aged do not get their proportional share of the nation's income (Item 11). Harris and Changas (1994) found similar results with the multiple-choice version. As for measuring bias against the aged, we found a net bias score of –19, which is somewhat higher than the score of –5 we found in these groups using the FAQ1 (Palmore, 1981a). Courtenay and Weidemann (1985) also found a relatively high net bias score of –17%,

TABLE 5.1 Percentage of Errors on the FAQ2 (true/false), by Item[a]

Item	% Errors[b]
1. Height declines	30
2. More chronic illness	8
3. Less acute illness	31
4. Fewer injuries in the home	49
5. Less absenteeism	22
6. Life expectancy same for blacks and whites	57
7. Life expectancy for women greater than for men	0
8. Medicare pays less than half of medical expenses	24
9. Social Security benefits increase with inflation	89
10. SSI guarantees minimum income	22
11. Aged get proportionate share of income	62
12. Lower rates of criminal victimization	51
13. More fearful of crime	27
14. Most law abiding	16
15. More widows than widowers	67
16. Aged vote less	27
17. More aged in public office	38
18. Proportion of Blacks growing	8
19. Participation in voluntary organizations stable	0
20. Majority live with others	51
21. Less poverty among aged	8
22. Poverty rate among aged Blacks 3 times that of whites	13
23. Disengaged less happy than active	0
24. "Empty nest" not cause of serious problems	81
25. Proportion widowed is decreasing	35

[a]All items presented In their "true" form.
[b]Mean: 33.
Source: Courtney & Weidmann, 1985.

even when the DK response was provided. Apparently the FAQ2 taps more negative beliefs than does the FAQ1.

RESULTS OF THE FAMHQ

As discussed in Chapter 3, a number of mental health professionals have suggested that a new quiz focused on mental health and illness among the aged would be useful in similar ways to the FAQ1 and FAQ2, that is, for measuring and increasing knowledge about mental health among the aged. Pruchno and Smyer (1983) developed a Mental Health Problems and Aging Quiz consisting of 18 true or false items. However, many of the items are ambiguous or controversial and cannot be conclusively documented by research. For example, the first item states, "Old age is a time of relative peace and tranquillity," which the test developers say is false. However, they cite only one source who claims it is false, but five sources who found it to be true. Part of the problem is that "relative peace and tranquillity" is a vague and ambiguous concept and hence difficult to verify. In addition to Pruchno and Smyer's quiz, there are also some unpublished tests in this area, but they have the same problems.

We developed the FAMHQ to avoid such ambiguities and controversies and to be more comprehensive; however, we are indebted to the previous quizzes for some of the ideas used in ours. It was designed to deal with the basic facts and misconceptions about mental illness and its treatment among the aged. As with the FAQ1 and FAQ2, the FAMHQ always stimulates much discussion because most people are surprised by many of the facts it contains. Because the true-false version is designed for self-scoring, participants can get immediate feedback on their misconceptions, which can be corrected by presentation and discussion of the correct facts.

A second use of the FAMHQ is to measure and compare different groups' levels of information about aging. For example, Table 5.2 shows that an undergraduate sociology class at Duke University had the lowest percentage of correct answers and the highest percentage of misconceptions. Because they had no exposure to gerontology, this result is to be expected. Notice that 58% correct is barely above the score that would be achieved by chance through random choices of true or false (50%). This shows that persons without any instruction in this field have little correct information about mental health among the aged.

The human behavior class was composed of first-year medical students who had had one lecture on gerontology and had taken and discussed the first two FAQs. They had slightly more correct and substantially fewer wrong answers, but the highest percentage DK (ignorance) answers. Apparently they had learned enough to be more aware of their ignorance in this area.

Health care professionals (Cole & Dancer, 1996) had means "above 70% correct," indicating considerable knowledge about aging and mental health. Nurses and aides in nursing homes had from 60% correct (aides) to 68% correct (registered nurses) (Swaykus, 1987).

TABLE 5.2 Responses to the FAMHQ (True/False Version), by Group

Group	% Correct	% Incorrect	% DK	No. of Subjects
Sociology class	58	27	15	23
Human behavior class	59	21	20	9
Gerontology class	65	21	14	46
Nurses and aides	60–68			137
Health care professionals	70+			200
Members of Southern Gerontological Society	72	23	5	29
Gerontology workshop	74	19	7	29
Means	66	22	12	473

The gerontology class had learned enough to get substantially more items correct (65%). The members of the Southern Gerontological Society who took the quiz as part of a lecture-demonstration got even more right (72%), and the participants in a workshop on religion and aging got the highest percentage correct of all (74%).

These differences support the validity of the quiz as a measure of knowledge in this area because one would expect those with more training and experience in this area to get more correct answers. It would be useful and interesting to find out how various age, sexual, religious, educational, and professional groups compare regarding correct information about aging and mental health.

A third use of the FAMHQ is to identify the most frequent misconceptions and areas of ignorance. Table 5.3 shows the combined results from the same 136 subjects described in the previous table. There were five items on which a majority were either mistaken or ignorant. In order of frequency, these were the following:

Item 12: 82% did not know that electroconvulsive therapy is safer and more effective for depression than medications*.

Item 20: 78% did not know that the majority of nursing home patients suffer from mental illness

Item 7: 69% did not know that fewer of the aged than the young have mental impairments.

---

*This item has been deleted in the revised version because it is rather controversial.

TABLE 5.3 Responses to the FAMHQ, by Item[a]

Item	% Correct	% Incorrect	% DK
1. Majority have mental illness	93	4	3
2. Cognitive impairment is inevitable	79	19	2
3. If false stories, point out lying	76	9	15
4. Neurosis and schizophrenia increase	63	22	15
5. Suicides increase for women	69	22	9
6. Suicides increase for men	58	30	12
7. Fewer aged than young have mental impairments	31	48	21
8. Primary problem is cognitive impairment	63	23	14
9. Alzheimer's is most common type	57	31	12
10. No cure for Alzheimer's	96	0	4
11. Alzheimer's patients all act the same	76	18	6
12. Medication safer for depression than Electro Convulsive Therapy	18	52	30
13. Best not to look at patient	91	3	6
14. Avoid talking to demented	99	0	1
15. Demented should not talk of past	93	0	7
16. Cognitive impairment increases	77	10	13
17. Brain impairment difficult to distinguish	58	19	23
18. Poor nutrition produces mental illness	69	18	13
19. More mental illness among lower socioeconomic groups	42	42	16
20. Majority nursing patients have mental illness	22	72	6
21. Elderly have fewer sleep problems	73	22	5
22. More depression among elderly than young	64	32	4
23. Widowhood more stressful for older women	46	51	3
24. More aged use mental services	70	21	9
25. Psychotherapy usually ineffective	71	22	7
Means	66	22	12

[a]All Items are presented as they appeared on the FAMHQ and may be either true or false.

Item 19: 58% did not know that mental illness is more common among lower socioeconomic groups.

Item 23: 54% did not know that widowhood is more stressful for younger women than older ones.

Conversely, most knew that the majority of older persons do not have mental illness (Item 1); that there is no cure for Alzheimer's disease

(Item 10); that it is all right to look at older mental patients (Item 13); that it is all right to talk to demented patients (Item 14); and that it is all right for demented patients to talk about their past (Item 15). (See also Swaykus, 1987.)

A final use of the FAMHQ would be to measure the effects of lectures, courses, or other training experiences by comparing before and after scores on the quiz. No one has done this to date, but I hope it will be done soon.

The multiple choice version of the FAMHQ has not yet been tested.

6

An Assessment of Uses of the FAQ1

Charles M. Barresi, Ph.D,[a]
and Timothy H. Brubaker, Ph.D[b]

Since its appearance in 1977, Palmore's Facts on Aging Quiz: Part 1 (FAQ1) has been used by many persons in a wide variety of settings. Some of these studies have generated a controversy within the literature, about the primary functions of the FAQ1. Although Palmore (1977) states that the primary objective of the FAQ is to measure knowledge about basic factual information in gerontology, it has been suggested by Klemmack (1978) that attitudes toward older people are measured by the FAQ1. Without a doubt, attitudinal measures have been confounded by knowledge questions in the "stereotype-about-old-age" literature (Brubaker & Powers, 1976). To evaluate the FAQ1, two primary questions need to be addressed: (a) Does the FAQ1 achieve the functions for which it was developed?; and (b) Does the FAQ1 measure knowledge about, or attitudes toward, old age?

This chapter presents the results of a survey we conducted, by questionnaire, of 25 known users of the FAQ1 (true/false version). We focused on several areas of inquiry:

1. The settings in which the quiz was used
2. The characteristics of the groups to whom the quiz was given

[a]From the Department of Sociology, University of Akron, Akron, Ohio; and [b]Department of Sociology, Miami University, Miami, Florida.

3. The stated objectives the users hoped to achieve in giving the quiz and how well they rated the quiz's ability to meet those objectives
4. Suggestions for revisions of the quiz
5. Suggestions for future use

In particular, we set out to examine how well the FAQ1 meets the four specific objectives outlined by Palmore (1977): (a) to stimulate discussion about old age, (b) to compare groups' levels of knowledge about old age, (c) to identify the most frequent misconceptions about old age, and (d) to measure indirectly a positive or negative bias toward old age. In addition, the issue of what is being measured is discussed.

The debate about the FAQ1 has developed as follows: Klemmack (1978), in a study using the quiz, states, "An individual's total score on the index would appear to be more a function of the negative (or positive) image of older persons than a function of level of information on aging" (p. 405). He concludes that the FAQ1 is not adequate as a research tool for assessing the level of knowledge about aging. Palmor (1978), in his reply to Klemmack, contends that the primary purpose of the FAQ1 is "edumetric" and that Klemmack is basing his conclusions on "psychometric" criteria. It should be noted that Klemmack's position is supported by Kamrass and Stevens (1979).

In another application of the FAQ1, Holtzman and Beck (1979) suggest that the FAQ does measure knowledge about old age. They found the FAQ to be adequate for achieving the first three objectives outlined by Palmore but also found it to be a poor measure of bias toward old age. Thus, they conclude, contrary to Klemmack, that the FAQ1 is an adequate measure of knowledge about old age and an inadequate measure of attitudes.

Because there is a controversy over the functions of the FAQ1, it is important to examine the validity of this quiz vis-à-vis the functions for which it was developed. Therefore, we developed a sample of users to whom we could put the primary questions raised about the quiz. A list of users of the FAQ1 was provided by Professor Palmore from a record of persons who wrote and stated that they were using it. To this list were added the names of all users who were known to us. In addition, the "snowball" technique of sampling was used by asking these subjects for the names and addresses of any other persons whom they knew had used the FAQ1. The combined lists included 41 persons.

A questionnaire with one follow-up was mailed out. This resulted in a yield of 25 usable questionnaires, 61% of the total. Our results will be discussed for each main area of inquiry.

SETTINGS FOR USE

Thirteen of the respondents used the FAQ1 in teaching settings (classroom and in-service training and workshops), and nine used the instrument in research, including master's theses, doctoral dissertations, and undergraduate and graduate courses. Three of the respondents reported using the FAQ1 in both research and teaching settings.

CHARACTERISTICS OF GROUPS TAKING THE QUIZ

The groups to whom the FAQ1 was administered varied in size and educational background. Size of the groups ranged from groups of 10 to 15 persons to very large groups of 250 to 300. The most frequent application was to groups in the 50-to-100 range. As shown in Table 6.1, groups were most often made up of undergraduate students (15 groups), followed next by nurses, agency staff personnel, and the general public (6 groups each). Less frequent applications were made to groups consisting of faculty members and nursing home residents.

TABLE 6.1 Group Composition, Number of Applications, and Mean Scores on the FAQ1

	Composition of Group	
	Number of Applications	Mean Score (%)
Undergraduates	15	56
Nurses	6	66
Agency personnel	6	62
General public	6	61
College faculty	1	62
High school faculty	1	61
High school students	1	54
Junior high school students	2	58
Nursing home residents	1	65

The mean scores on the quiz achieved by the various groups are also reported in Table 6.1. The average scores range from a high of 66%, attained by nurses, to a low of 54%, attained by the high school students. The mean score of all undergraduate groups is 56%, which is lower than several other groups, including general public groups, which had a mean score of 61%. A college faculty group of home economics department members scored 62%, and a group of high school faculty scored 61%. Overall the reported mean scores from the various applications were not impressive, when one considers that a 50% score can be attributed to chance factors alone. Out of more than 40 applications of the FAQ1 with students, faculty, professionals, and general public groups, the highest score reported was only 6,996 (17 correct responses out of 25). The lowest score, 35%, was reported for a group of undergraduate student nurses. This score indicates a little under 9 correct responses out of 25.

OBJECTIVES FOR USE

One of the main purposes of this survey of FAQ1 users is to determine whether or not Palmore's (1977) stated objectives for the use of the FAQ1 are being met by current users.

Table 6.2 summarizes the objectives that respondents sought to meet through the use of the FAQ1. The users listed their objectives in response to an open-ended question. By far the largest number of responses (33%) indicated that the objective of using the quiz was to measure and compare information about aging. In 16% of the applications, the quiz was used to measure bias toward the aged, and in 10% it was used to stimulate discussion. An additional 8% of the applications were for measuring misconceptions about aging. Thus, 34 out of a total of 51 responses, or 67%, were in concert with the objectives Palmore (1977) originally identified as uses for the FAQ1.

The remaining 33% of the responses were for objectives that were not anticipated by Palmore, and most relate to attitudinal dimensions. Some of these objectives are highly questionable ones, such as transmitting information about aging and changing attitudes toward the elderly. Others are more plausible objectives and are in reality extensions of the use of the FAQ1 as a research tool, such as for measuring relationships between

TABLE 6.2 Objectives That Respondents Sought to Meet With the FAQ1[a]

Objective	No. of Responses	% of Responses
Measure and compare information about aging	17	33
Measure bias toward the aged	8	16
Stimulate discussion	5	10
Transmit information about aging	5	10
Measure misconceptions about aging	4	8
Measure relationship between knowledge and other variables (demographic data, beliefs)	3	6
Measure relationship between knowledge and attitudes toward the elderly	2	4
Measure attitudes toward the elderly	1	2
Change attitudes toward the elderly	1	2
Determine content areas for in-service training	1	2
Evaluate the FAQ1	1	2

[a] Note that, although the number of respondents was 25, the total number of responses was 51 because many respondents gave multiple answers.

knowledge and other variables and between knowledge and attitudes toward the elderly, or for determining the content areas for in-service training. Indeed, these latter uses, although not mentioned by Palmore (1977), are ones that are commonly employed in ongoing research and constitute imaginative and useful extensions of the FAQ1's worth to the field of gerontology.

EVALUATION OF SUCCESS IN MEETING OBJECTIVES

Respondents were asked to rate each of the objectives originally stated by Palmore (1977), in view of their experience with the FAQ1. Each of the four objectives was rated on a scale of 1 (does not meet this objective) to 5 (does meet this objective). The results are summarized in Table 6.3. The objective that is most positively endorsed is that the FAQ1 stimulates group discussion about aging. All of the respondents rated it either a 4 or 5. The second objective, which is to measure and compare different groups' levels of knowledge about aging, was positively endorsed (4 or 5) by 72% of the respondents, while the remaining 28% rated it as neutral (3). Use of the quiz to help identify persons'

TABLE 6.3 Respondents' Rating of Palmore's Objectives for the FAQ1, on a Scale of 1 (Does Not Meet Objective) to 5 (Does Meet Objective)

Objective	1	2	3	4	5	Total[a]
1. The FAQ1 stimulates group discussion about aging.				N = 3 (14%)	N = 19 (86%)	N = 22 (100%)
2. The FAQ1 can be used to measure and compare different groups' levels of knowledge about aging.			N = 7 (28%)	N = 4 (16%)	N = 14 (56%)	N = 25 (100%)
3. The FAQ1 helps identify persons' most frequent misconceptions about aging.		N = 1 (4%)	N = 3 (14%)	N = 4 (18%)	N = 14 (64%)	N = 22 (100%)
4. The FAQ1 indirectly measures a positive or negative bias toward the aged.	N = 3 (15%)	N = 3 (15%)	N = 5 (25%)	N = 5 (25%)	N = 4 (20%)	N = 20 (100%)

[a]Total N does not include the "no answer" or "not relevant" (to the user's purposes) category.

most frequent misconceptions about aging was rated positively (4 or 5) by 82%, 14% are neutral (3), and only one person rated it negatively (2). The last objective, measurement of bias, was rated positively by only 45% of the respondents, and 25% were neutral and 30% rated it negatively (1 or 2). The respondents also found this fourth objective the least useful because 20% of them failed to rate the objective at all, for various reasons. Their comments included "not relevant" and "not applicable to my use." This finding supports Holtzman and Beck's (1979) criticism that the use of the FAQ1 as an indirect measure of bias is not justified.

Open-ended responses to a general evaluation question regarding the FAQ1 were positive in a ratio of about three to one. Seventy-six percent of the respondents found the FAQ to be a useful tool for measuring knowledge and misconceptions about aging, for both teaching and research purposes. Its major value seems to lie in the fact that it is easy to administer and score and is economical to reproduce.

Approximately one quarter of the respondents (24%) were negative in their general evaluation of the FAQ1 and cited criticisms that dealt mainly with the content and nature of the items and their inability to measure bias or misconceptions adequately. Some critics considered the instrument as useful only with novice groups, others contended it was too difficult and culture-bound for many groups. The greatest number of negative comments dealt with the wording or phrasing of some items that were considered confusing or to contain objectionable terms (e.g., "demented" in Item 1). An additional criticism was the lack of items in areas judged to be important, such as life review and creativity of older persons.

SUGGESTED REVISIONS

The users of the FAQ1 were queried regarding their suggestions for revision of the instrument. They suggested that it include new items that deal with the aging of minorities and women and the behavioral consequences of the loss of sensory perception (e.g., hearing). Other suggestions focus on the rewording of items to reduce confusion or vagueness (specific items mentioned were 16, 24, and 25). Another user stated that rank-order correlation of the separate items showed that items 11 and 25 had no uniformity of response for any of the three studies in which he did rank-order correlations. Other item revisions suggested are to eliminate specific percentage references in true-false questions and to randomize the order of the items so as to prevent test persons from guessing the correct answers based on the alternation of true and false items.

A few respondents would like to see the items standardized and subjected to appropriate statistical analysis so that the validity of the items could be established. Others would revise the nature of the instrument completely and use multiple-choice or short open-ended answers rather than true-false responses. Another suggestion is to separate the FAQ1 into separate sections dealing with the biological, psychological, and social aspects of aging, which could be used separately to test better those groups with specialized training (see Barresi & Brubaker [1979], for suggested categories for FAQ1 items). A simplified version for children and less educated adults is also suggested.

Several respondents addressed the use of the FAQ1 to measure bias and suggested revisions in regard to this objective of the test. These suggestions essentially call for a reexamination of the bias direction of the items. Several of them call into question especially those items that deal with percentage distribution of various characteristics arguing that ignorance about percentages does not necessarily show bias. One respondent suggested that a solution to this issue would be to construct a separate instrument to measure bias toward the elderly that could be administered in conjunction with the FAQ1.

SUGGESTIONS FOR FUTURE USE OF THE FAQ1

Finally, this survey asked respondents for suggestions for future uses of the quiz, including such things as types of audiences or techniques of administration. A major category of response was the suggestion to broaden the administration of the FAQ1 to include more groups in the general population as well as some specific groups, such as Veterans Administration counselors and service providers in state agencies. Several respondents suggested the use of the FAQ 1 for persons who have direct contact with elderly, such as health care personnel and children of elderly parents. Many suggested the use of the instrument in pretest-posttest situations, to determine the learning that occurs in classroom and workshop settings or through extensive contact with the elderly.

Several respondents called for wider publication of the quiz including one who believed it would be a good idea to use it as part of a television documentary to increase knowledge and awareness about aging in the general population. One person suggested using the FAQ1 as part of a longer questionnaire that would include a "previous-contact-with-the-elderly scale," the McKillip Career Interest in Gerontology Scale, and the Rosencranz and McNevin Aging Semantic Differential Scale.

Finally, a general suggestion made by several users was to establish baseline scores so that comparisons could be made between groups in the general population by age, sex, race, occupation, and level of education. This would necessitate wider applications and continued statistical analysis and validation.

SUMMARY

This survey of users of the FAQ1 indicates that it is being widely used in gerontology education and research and is being administered to many groups, including students, health professionals, and teachers. The respondents are generally using the quiz for the purposes originally stated by Palmore (1977), but several of them are extending these objectives beyond those originally stated. In fact, some of these uses are highly dubious and have been called into question by critics of the quiz. An assessment of the four original objectives reveals that users are highly positive about three out of four. Less than half of the sample, however, find that the FAQ1 meets the fourth objective, that of indirectly measuring bias toward the aged.

Suggested revisions center mainly on item revision and the inclusion of new items. As might be expected from the general concern regarding the measure of bias, many of the suggestions call for revisions that would strengthen this objective of the quiz. Suggestions for future use of the FAQ1 deal mainly with wider publication and use of the quiz to establish baseline scores for various groups. Other suggestions would see the quiz used as part of a longer instrument that would include other published scales and the establishment of more sophisticated statistical analysis of the results of FAQ1 scores and their correlates. There appears to be consensus that the FAQ1 adequately measures knowledge about old age. Attitudes toward old age, however, are not measured by the quiz; therefore, users should consider their own objectives before the quiz is selected. If knowledge is to be measured, then the FAQ1 is appropriate; if attitudes are sought, then it is not. To facilitate the use of the quiz, we suggest (a) periodic revisions to update the items to reflect changes in the older populations; (b) publication of scores from various educational and professional groups, to establish baseline data; and (c) development of attitudinal measures to be used with the quiz in measuring attitudes toward old age.

7

Summary and Future Directions

SUMMARY

Development

The FAQs had a modest beginning as a way of stimulating student interest in a course on aging in 1976. During the following decade, the FAQ1 became the international standard for measuring knowledge and misconceptions about aging. By 1987, over 90 studies had used it on a wide variety of groups. It has been criticized and defended. Many revisions have been suggested, and several have been incorporated in the current version.

Because of the popularity of the FAQ1, an alternate form, the FAQ2, was developed to be used either in a test-retest situation or as an additional test of more knowledge and misconceptions. A third quiz, the FAMHQ, was also developed to focus on knowledge about mental health aspects of aging.

A multiple-choice version of the FAQ2 was developed and tested in 1994, and a multiple-choice version of the FAQ1 was developed and tested in 1996. Both were found to be significantly more reliable than the true/false versions, even though they take longer to administer than the true/false versions. I developed a multiple-choice version of the FAMHQ for publication in this edition. This version has not yet been tested.

The first three chapters of this book present the revised three quizzes, both the true/false and the multiple-choice versions, and their updated documentation.

The revisions were made to make the items simpler and easier to understand and provide a DK response option. Provision of the DK option improves the quizzes in several ways by reducing guessing, improving reliability, making the scores on FAQ 1 and FAQ2 similar, and allowing a distinction between a misconception (an erroneous answer) and ignorance (a DK response).

Uses

The fourth chapter of this book provides instructions for the four main uses of the quizzes: to educate, measure learning, test knowledge, and measure attitudes. Educational uses include stimulating interest and discussion, correcting misconceptions, and providing information about aging. For this usage, students can score their own quizzes and compare their scores to norms for various groups. However, for measuring learning the quiz must be more carefully administered, and self-scoring is not recommended.

To measure learning, the same quiz may be repeated after the learning experience if the correct answers are not given in between administrations. The preferable method, however, is to use the alternate forms (FAQ1 and FAQ2) before and after the learning experience, to minimize practice effects and other problems with repeating the same quiz.

When testing knowledge for comparisons between groups, it is also important to administer the quiz carefully and not allow self-scoring. Otherwise, apparent differences between groups may be due to differences in the administration and/or inaccuracy of the self-scoring.

For research purposes, we recommend the use of the multiple-choice versions because we found them to be more reliable than the true/false versions. The FAQs are not recommended as the best way of measuring attitudes toward the aged; however, if time and expense prohibit using one of the more direct measures, it is possible to compute scores that indirectly measure positive, negative, and net bias toward the aged.

The Psychological Facts on Aging Quiz is a combination of items from the FAQ1 and FAQ2, plus two original items by McCutcheon

(1986). It deals with psychological and sociological facts about aging. This quiz may be useful for those who want to focus on these aspects of aging, either in instruction or in measurement.

Major Findings

The major findings of the studies using the FAQs and FAMHQ studies are presented in Chapter 5. We will summarize these findings in the form of 13 propositions about knowledge and attitudes toward aging. These propositions are subject to revision by findings from future research, but they represent the present state of our knowledge.

1. The average person with a high-school education has almost as many misconceptions as correct items of information about aging.
2. The average person with some college education has misconceptions on about one-third of the items.
3. The average person with at least a college-level course in gerontology gets over 80% of the items in the FAQ1 and FAQ2 correct.
4. The most frequent misconceptions, with a majority of respondents not knowing the correct answer, includes 2 biological items (FAQ2 Items 4 and 6); 7 psychological items (FAQ1 Items 11, 16, and 24 and FAMHQ Items 7, 12, 19, and 20); and 12 socioeconomic items (FAQ1 Items 7, 19, 21, and 23; FAQ2 Items 9 to 12, 15, 20, and 24; and FAMHQ Item 23).
5. The average person tends to have more anti-aged bias than pro-aged bias.
6. Bias toward the aged is associated with lack of knowledge about the aged.
7. The FAQ1 can measure learning about aging.
8. Both knowledge levels and the most frequent misconceptions tend to be similar in all the countries studied.
9. Knowledge levels tend to be similar in all age, sex, and racial groups. The only variables consistently related to knowledge levels are education and attitudes toward the aged.
10. Intergroup and test-retest reliability on the FAQ1 is relatively high. Reliability is even higher with the multiple-choice versions.
11. The face validity of the items is established by the research cited in the documentation.

12. Edumetric rather than psychometric criteria should be used in evaluating these quizzes.
13. Results from the FAQ1 and the FAQ2 (with a DK option) are similar enough to allow their usage as alternate measures of knowledge.

Survey of Users

A survey of 25 users of the FAQ1, presented in Chapter 6, found consensus that the quiz is a good stimulus for group discussion about aging; that it can be used to measure and compare different groups' levels of knowledge about aging; and that it helps identify the most frequent misconceptions about aging.

There was an almost even split as to whether the quiz was useful as an indirect measure of bias toward the aged.

There were several suggested revisions, centering mainly on item revision, reorganization of the order of presentation, and the inclusion of new items. Suggestions for future uses of the quiz included administration to more groups in the general population as well as some specific groups. Others suggested more use in pretest-posttest situations. Several users also suggested wider publication of the FAQ.

FUTURE DIRECTIONS

Policy Implications

Perhaps the most important general finding from these studies is that most people without training in gerontology have many negative misconceptions about the aged. This is true regardless of sex, age, occupation, or most other characteristics, the one known exception being education. This is further evidence of the ageism that pervades our culture and the modern Western world (Palmore, 1990). This ageism is expressed in both the prejudice reflected in the negative misconceptions documented by these studies and the discrimination that flows from this prejudice including employment discrimination, the tendency to avoid and exclude the aged, the lack of adequate medical care, and the lack of social and psychological services. One of the most tragic forms of discrimination against the aged is the tendency of many medical and other service professions to discount symptoms and problems among the aged because of the belief that they are "just part of growing older."

Medical and other service professionals are particularly vulnerable to these negative misconceptions about the aged because they tend to generalize from the sick and needy aged they most often serve, assuming that the symptoms and problems they see among their patients are simply "normal" among the aged and that little or nothing can be done about them. Therefore, they do not treat or attempt to help the aged patient as vigorously as they would a younger patient. This tends to become a self-fulfilling prophecy and forms a vicious circle in which the negative attitude is confirmed by the discriminatory behavior. This process is well known in the areas of racism and sexism, but is just as detrimental in the area of ageism. To combat this ageism and its pernicious effects, we need more education and information about the true facts on aging among all age and educational groups in our society. We need to integrate learning about aging into grade school curricula, along with information that combats racism and sexism. High schools should include segments on aging in their biology and social science courses. Basic college courses in biology, psychology, and the social sciences should include sections on aging. There should also be available more advanced courses in social gerontology, psychology of aging, biology of aging, and so forth. Especially in professional schools that train practitioners who work with the aged, such as doctors, lawyers, social workers, psychologists, and ministers, there should be required curricula on the special needs and resources of the aged. The FAQs can be useful in all these learning experiences, to stimulate interest, identify and correct misconceptions, and measure learning.

In addition to the inclusion of gerontology in formal educational experiences, those who have left school also need to correct their misconceptions and learn more facts about aging. This could be done through adult education courses, television and radio shows, magazine and newspaper articles, church and synagogue programs, civic club programs, celebration of Senior Citizens Month, and so on. Some of this has already begun, so ageism may already be on the decline in our society; however, the results of the FAQs make it clear that there is still much ageism left.

Here, too, the FAQs could be useful. Selected items from the FAQ1 have been used for a television educational video cassette (Courtenay &

Suhart, 1980). Other television "talk" shows have been produced using items from the FAQ1, and they have formed the basis for numerous newspaper and magazine articles. One appeared in *USA Today*, which used 10 items from the FAMHQ (Johnson, 1986).

These uses of the FAQs by the media show that there is widespread public interest in aging in general and in this format specifically for gaining information about aging. If local and national groups would urge more media to do more features using the FAQs and other methods of correcting negative stereotypes about the aged, we could make substantial progress toward overcoming ageism in our society.

Future Research

The FAQ1 has been administered to enough groups so that we have fairly good standards for mean scores by educational level. Moreover, we know that there are no consistent differences in terms of other demographic variables. In contrast, there have been few studies using the FAQ2, and there is only our pretesting of the FAMHQ. Thus, there is a pressing need to do the same kinds of testing with these two quizzes as have been done with the first quiz. Also the multiple-choice versions need to be tested on groups other than those used in the original test at the University of Tennessee.

There also needs to be more testing of all three quizzes, using edumetric criteria outlined by Carver (1974). As indicated previously, psychometric criteria are inappropriate for these quizzes, but edumetric criteria are appropriate when one wants to measure learning about aging. Specifically, the edumetric efficiency of the items could be examined to see which ones are the most sensitive measures of learning, that is, which items show the largest gain in correct answers in before-and-after tests. The edumetric reliability of alternate forms of the quizzes also could be examined by measuring the consistency of gain in scores within the individual, that is, determining whether or not the gain in score remains at a second follow-up test. Using these criteria, one might construct a third FAQ for measuring learning, which would combine the best edumetric items from the other two FAQs and the FAMHQ.

Another area for future research is the translation into other languages and testing the quizzes in other countries. Although the quiz has been translated into two other languages (Japanese and French) and used in several other countries, we know nothing about knowledge levels in most countries. When the quiz is translated, care should be taken to make the translation as accurate and valid as possible. First of all, the validity of the items for the given country needs to be checked because the facts about aging will vary somewhat in different countries. Second, some procedure for checking on the accuracy of the translation should be used. For example, one widely used procedure is to have one person translate the document into the foreign language and then have another person translate the translation back into English, to see how closely it compares with the original. Any discrepancy needs to be cleared up, perhaps by a committee of translators, to avoid the bias of one or even two translators.

Another idea for future research is to replicate studies using the FAQ1 that were done about 20 years ago to measure change in knowledge levels. One might expect there would be some increase in knowledge as a result of all the education and public dissemination of information about aging that have occurred in the past two decades. One would need to test groups that are as similar as possible to those in the original studies to conclude that differences in results between the earlier and later studies are due to increases in knowledge rather than to differences in the groups compared.

FAQ Game

A final idea for future development of the FAQs is to create a game using the facts in the quizzes. A simple form of such a game would be to make a set of cards with a true-false or multiple-choice question on one side of the card and the answer on the other side. Then players (or teams) could take turns drawing a card to answer. If the player gets the correct answer they get to keep the card. Otherwise, the card would be put at the bottom of the stack. When all the cards are correctly answered, the player with the most cards wins the game.

A more complicated version could be a board game. The throwing of a die would determine which type of question the player must answer similar to the "Trivial Pursuit" format. In either case, making a game out of the quizzes would be an entertaining and possibly popular way of learning about aging and correcting misconceptions.

Part II

Studies Using the Facts on Aging Quiz: Abstracts

Introduction

We have summarized in Chapter 5 the main research findings relevant to knowledge levels, bias, validity, and reliability. In this part of the book we will give the complete reference and summarize the purpose, sample, main findings, and conclusions of each study using the FAQs that has been reported to me or that has been listed in the standard periodical indexes.

If one wants further information about a study, one may look up the original publication (for the published studies). For unpublished studies, I may be able to forward your inquiry to the author, although some of our addresses are no longer valid. Also, I may be able to answer your question on the basis of the report I have, or I may be able to reproduce the report for you. For such inquiries, please enclose a self-addressed and stamped envelope for my reply.

We have included abstracts of all the studies we know of, as of June 1997. For published studies since then, we recommend checking the standard periodical indexes such as MEDLINE (computer based) or Social Sciences Citation Index.

The abstracts are arranged alphabetically by first author's last name. Also, their subjects are included in the index, so one can use the index to look up all the studies on a given subject.

Abstracts

Adelman, R. & Albert, R. (1987). Medical students' attitudes toward the elderly. *Gerontology and Geriatrics Education, 7*, 141–155.

Reviews instruments used and findings of several studies of medical students attitudes toward the elderly, including studies using the FAQ1 and FAQ2.

Allen, B. (1981). Knowledge of aging: A cross-sectional study of three different age groups. *Educational Gerontology, 6*, 49.

A study was conducted to determine the factual accuracy of youngsters' knowledge about older people and the moderating effect on knowledge resulting from differences in age/education, sex, racial origin, and experience living in a household with an older person. The 208 youngsters were drawn from middle schools, high schools, and a college in three Florida counties. The FAQ1 was administered, overall and item error rates determined, and comparative analyses made for each of the four hypothesized moderator variables.

The mean percentage correct for college students (59%) was slightly higher than that of the two younger groups (54% and 55%), but this difference was not significant. The majority of all three groups had errors on eight items: 7, 11, 16, 19, 20, 21, 23, and 24. The average percentage correct on these items was from 30% to 38%. Age and education had little effect in developing accurate knowledge about older people. There were also no significant differences in total mean percentage correct by sex, race, or experience living in a household with an older person.

There were a few significant differences between these groups on some specific items, but this would be expected to occur by chance, with so many comparisons. There was a negative net bias in all three age/education groups, ranging from –18 for the high school students to –10 for the college students. Differences in negative net bias between the other groupings were not striking. There is evident need for more accurate knowledge on the part of U.S. youth about the growing segment of older persons in the population.

Anonymous. (1986). *Negatively biased misconceptions about old age and aging in Japanese adults.* Unpublished manuscript. Tokyo, Japan: Tokyo Metropolitan Institute of Gerontology.

Knowledge about aging was measured using the FAQ1 with a sample of 555 adults living in Tokyo, aged 30 to 59 years. The total percentage correct and the net aged bias were analyzed for associations with demographic variables. The total percentage correct (57%) was comparable with previous studies of adults in the United States. College-educated people had significantly higher scores than others, but no other variables were related to knowledge.

The aged net bias score was strongly negative (–38) and was significantly higher in the noncollege educated. This strongly negative score is substantially higher than those reported in previous studies for other countries. This appears to be contrary to Palmore's (1985) observations of greater respect for the aged and aging among Japanese adults.

Palmore may have observed normative meanings underlying Japanese traditional rituals of respect for the elderly, whereas his FAQ1 may measure actual negative feelings about aging in Japanese adults.

Anonymous. (1992). Effects of a geriatric course on knowledge about aging among optometry students. Unpublished manuscript submitted to *The Gerontologist.*

The FAQ1 was administered to two classes of optometry students. One class experienced a geriatric course and clinic concurrently; the other class experienced a geriatric clinic prior to the course. Scores increased significantly after the experience for both classes. Exposure to geriatric patients before didactic instruction did not improve pretest scores; however, the number of patient exposures was significantly and positively related to the FAQ scores at post-test. Also anti-age bias was reduced at post-test.

Ansello, E., & Lamy, P. (1987). *Geropharmacy and gerontology for rural community pharmacists.* Unpublished report to the AARP Andrus Foundation from the Center on Aging, University of Maryland, College Park, MD.

Pharmacists were given training in geropharmacy and gerontology in three formats: weekly, weekend, and monthly. The FAQ1 was administered before and after the training sessions. The weekly and weekend formats produced more knowledge gains than the monthly format. The mean percentage correct scores before training were about 68% and the after training scores were about 76%.

Ausherman, J. (1991). Junior high school health teachers' knowledge and attitudes about aging and implementation of aging education. *Educational Gerontology, 17*, 391–401.

The FAQ1 (with DK option) was administered to 304 health teachers in North Carolina. These teachers exhibit a moderately low level of knowledge and a slightly positive attitude toward the aged. Knowledge of aging was positively related to their attitudes toward the aged ($r = .19$). Knowledge was also related to implementation of aging education. Neither gender, age, nor race makes a difference in knowledge or attitudes. Although these teachers are expected to teach aging education according to the Basic Education Plan, they lack important knowledge about the topic.

Barnet, M. (1979). *Contact with elderly persons as a correlate of knowledge about aging.* Unpublished master's thesis, Boston: Boston University.

The purpose of the study was to compare knowledge of aging as measured by the FAQ1 with the variables of age, sex, disciplinary background, educational level, and contact with elderly persons. The sample consisted of 129 staff members of a community mental health center including both professional and business and clerical staff. Disciplinary backgrounds represented included medicine; education; nursing; psychology; social work; art, movement, and occupational therapy; counseling; and "other."

Educational level ranged from high school graduate to doctor. Age range was 20 to 65 years.

The mean score for all subjects was 64% correct. Items on which a majority had incorrect answers were 2, 7, 12, 16, 17, 19, 21, and 24 (Item 23 was not tallied because of a typographical error).

Analysis showed no significant relationship between knowledge of aging and the variables of age, sex, disciplinary background, or educational level. There was a significant positive correlation ($r = .18$; $p < .05$) between knowledge and contact with the elderly.

Barresi, C., & Brubaker, T. (1979). Clinical social workers' knowledge about aging: Responses to the "Facts on Aging Quiz." *Journal of Gerontological Social Work, 2*, 137–146.

This study explores clinical social workers' knowledge about old age, using the FAQ1. Data are based on a mailed questionnaire completed by 200 social workers in Ohio with master of social work degrees. The average percentage of correct responses was 68%. Analysis of items on which 60% or less of the respondents answered correctly reveals five items that indicate a negative bias (7, 16, 17, 21, and 24), three with a positive bias (2, 4, and 12), and two neutral (19 and 23). Rank ordering of the content areas most often missed indicates sociology of aging and demography of aging are the two areas where knowledge is most lacking. Implications for graduate education and in-service training for clinical social workers are discussed.

Belgrave, L., Lavin, B., Breslau, N., & Haug, M. (1982). Stereotyping of the aged by medical students. *Gerontology and Geriatrics Education, 3*, 37–44.

This research focuses on negative stereotypes of a sample of medical students (N = 120). Fifteen items from the FAQ1 were used to form a negative stereotyping score.

The mean stereotyping score was 5.3 (out of a possible 15). The higher the score, the greater the negative stereotyping. There was a trend toward lower stereotyping scores by those choosing the primary care specialties of family practice and internal medicine, as compared to surgery. Other specialties (obstetrics-gynecology and psychiatry) had scores similar to the primary care specialties. Also, students who chose medicine mainly as offering a chance to help others were less likely (mean = 4.1) than others to have high stereotyping scores. Similarly, students at the school emphasizing research and specialization were more likely to have higher stereotyping scores than those at the community-oriented school (means were 5.7 and 3.8, respectively).

There was no significant relationship between preferred location and stereotyping. There was no meaningful relationship between the stereotyping scores and sex, race, general orientation to authority, or Medical College Aptitude Test scores.

When a stepwise multiple regression was employed on the stereotyping scores, the type of school entered first, the reasons for choosing medicine entered second, and preference for primary care specialty entered third. Although the last two variables did not meet usual statistical significance levels (p = .05), they did contribute more than 1% to explained variance and were therefore retained in the regression equation. These three variables together explained 17% of the variance.

Blackwell, D. (1979, January 22). *Effects of a workshop on aging on knowledge about aging.* Unpublished letter to E. Palmore.

FAQ1 Items 1, 2, 4, 10, 12, 15, and 20 were used in pretest and posttest formats to measure the effects of a workshop on aging on four groups of persons working with the aged: (a) nurse's aides in a nursing home (N = 15); (b) home health aides caring for aged persons (N = 43); (c) professionals working in mental health centers and providing services to the aged (N = 59); and (d) professionals and paraprofessionals working in the Office of Family Security, State Bureau of Aging Services, or for the parish councils on aging (N = 107).

In the first and second groups, only Item 20 had a significant increase in percentage correct after the workshop. In the third group, Items 1 and 11 had significant increases. In the fourth group, Items 2, 4, and 20 had significant increases.

Bond, S. (1979, January 28). *Knowledge about aging among participants in retirement planning courses.* Unpublished letter to E. Palmore.

The FAQ1 was given to participants in three retirement planning courses at the University of Manitoba, Winnipeg. Twenty were students in a retirement planning course offered as part of a certificate program in gerontology (average age, 36); 22 were participants in a preretirement program (average age, 62); and 15 were participants in a retirement planning seminar for personnel officers (average age, 45). The FAQ1 was modified to correspond to Canadian data.

The three groups had mean scores of 80%, 68%, and 76% correct, respectively, indicating that the students in the gerontology program knew the most about aging.

Bressler, D. (1996). *Occupational therapists' knowledge on aging.* Master's thesis, Levin School of Health sciences, Touro College.

This study assessed the level of knowledge of aging among registered occupational therapists (OT) in New York State and determined the factors that influence knowledge of aging in this group. The FAQ1 was mailed to 200 OTs and 116 (58%) responded. Results indicated that OTs have knowledge of aging equivalent to other allied health professionals. OTs who specialize in geriatrics do not demonstrate a statistically significant difference from other health professionals in their correct responses to the FAQ1.

Broder, H., & Block, M. (1986, July-August). Effects of geriatric education on the knowledge of dental students. *Special Care in Dentistry,* 177–179.

The FAQ1 was administered before and 1 to 2 years after a geriatric course for two classes of dental students (N = 135). The average percentage correct was 68% on the pretest. A majority of the students missed Items 7, 12, 16, 19, 21, 23 to 25 on the pretest. On the posttest, no items were missed by a majority.

There was a significant positive change from the pretest to the posttest immediately after the course (from 68% to 94%). However, scores declined significantly during 1 and 2 years after the course (to 76% correct). This indicates that some of the material learned during the course was forgotten later.

Brown, I. (1993). *Ageism in American culture: Patterns of prejudice and discrimination by the dominant group and its effects on older African-Americans.* Ph.D. dissertation, Union Institute Graduate School, Cincinnati, OH.

A total of 114 white residents of Prince George County, MD, were surveyed using the FAQ1 and the Old People scale. Analysis showed that ageism is still prevalent in American culture and that certain misconceptions about older African Americans are more pronounced in certain age groups. Racism and ageism caused older African Americans to suffer from the "double-jeopardy factor." African American females suffer from sexism, which also causes "triple jeopardy."

Brubaker, T., & Barresi, C. (1979). Social workers' level of knowledge about old age and perceptions of service delivery to the elderly. *Research on Aging, 1*, 213–232.

Following the assumption that practitioners' levels of knowledge and perceptions of their clients' characteristics affect the delivery of services, 200 clinical social workers were questioned regarding knowledge of and attitudes toward elderly persons. The FAQ1 was used to classify respondents' knowledge as high or low. There were also 19 items that focused on attitudes toward service delivery to the elderly.

There was no significant difference in knowledge by sex, but age was significantly related to more knowledge ($r = .17$), and this relationship was stronger for the 55- to 71-year-old group. There was no significant relationship between knowledge and years with an M.S.W., nor with having gerontology courses. There were few significant relationships between knowledge and attitudes toward service delivery. When age was controlled, there were significant relationships between higher knowledge and disagreement with a free annual medical checkup for persons over 60; and between higher knowledge and disagreement with the need for special community and professional groups to advocate special interests for the elderly. It appears that there was a tendency for more knowledgeable social workers to believe that government services to the elderly should not be viewed as unique for this age group.

However, the lack of many clear differences in attitudes between those with high and low knowledge suggests that an accurate knowledge base is not a primary factor in the perception of service delivery to the elderly.

Burris, R. (1992). Measuring the learning outcomes of a continuing education seminar about the aging process on the knowledge level of registered nurses. *Dissertation Abstracts International, 53* (12-A), 4169.

The FAQ1 and FAQ2 were used to assess the learning about aging in a continuing education seminar. Thirty-four licensed registered nurses were in the seminar, and 33 were in a comparison group. Nurses in the comparison group answered an average of 58% correct, and those in the experimental group answered an average of 78% correct. No other variables (age, gender, education, previous gerontological training) had a significant effect on knowledge. An analysis of internal consistency reliability found a Cronbach's coefficient alpha of .86.

Byrd, M. (1984). Personal growth aspects of peer counselor training for older adults. *Educational Gerontology, 10*, 369–385.

Although there has been an increase in the use of older adults as peer counselors, little is known about the effects of such training on the peer counselor students. The present study sought to examine the degree of personal growth experienced by older adult participants of a peer counselor training course. The study included 38 older adult peer counselor students and 59 controls. The participants were tested with three types of measures. The first type, psychological functioning, included Palmore's FAQ1 (1977), Neugarten, Havighurst, and Tobin's Life Satisfaction Index (1961), and Lawton's Philadelphia Geriatric Center Morale Scale (1975). Also used were Wessman and Ricks's (1965) 16-item Personal Feeling Scale and Lieberman et al.'s (1973) scales for measuring encounter group effectiveness and assessing methods older adults typically use to solve their personal problems.

The FAQ1 scores had a significant increase in the posttest (from 13 to 24 correct). There were no significant changes in the life satisfaction or morale scores. However, the training course did significantly increase levels of self-confidence and -reliance.

Carmel, S., Cwikel, J., & Galinody, D. (1992). Changes in knowledge, attitudes, and work preferences following courses in gerontology among medical, nursing, and social work students. *Educational Gerontology, 18*, 329–342.

Evaluated the effects of courses in gerontology and geriatrics on knowledge, attitudes, and work preferences among medical (n = 47), nursing (n = 28), and social work students (n = 19) in Israel. Nursing and social work students increased their average percent correct on the FAQ1 from

55 and 52, respectively, to 63 and 64, respectively. There was no significant change among the medical students (61% correct). There were no significant attitude nor work preference changes. There were no significant correlations between knowledge, attitudes, and work preferences.

Carmel, S., Galinsky, D., & Cwikel, J. (1990). Knowledge, attitudes, and work preferences regarding the elderly among medical students and practicing physicians. *Behavior, Health, & Aging, 1*, 99–104.

Examined knowledge about the elderly and its relation to attitudes and preferences for work with the elderly among 170 medical students and practicing physicians (PPs). Subjects (Ss) completed questionnaires including the FAQ. Students and PPs did not differ on general knowledge about the elderly and their negative attitudes toward the elderly. Increases in knowledge about gerontology did not necessarily have positive effects on attitudes and on the willingness to work with the elderly. Actual work experience, however, especially among family physicians, had a positive effect on the willingness to continue to work with the elderly.

Chandler, J. Rachal, J., & Kazelskis, R. (1986). *Attitudes of long-term care nursing personnel toward the elderly*. Unpublished letter to E. Palmore.

The FAQ2 and Kogan's Old People (OP) scale were administered to nurses in two long-term care facilities located on the Gulf Coast of the Mississippi. An experimental group was given an experiential education program about aging. The program had no significant effect on attitudes. The registered nurses had more positive attitudes than the licensed practical nurses and nurse aides.

Clark, M. (1996). Measuring facts and views of aging with Palmore's quizzes. Abstract in *The Gerontologist, 36*, 1: (Special Issue), 375.

FAQ1 and FAQ2 were combined and simultaneously completed by 311 undergraduate students, with a "don't know" option allowed. Reliability analyses indicate that this addition option contributed to the comparability of the two quizzes in terms of knowledge and attitudes. The FAQ2 showed significantly lower % correct and greater % DK, but no significant difference in % wrong. The FAQ2 showed significantly higher pro-aging and anti-aging biases, but no significant difference in net bias scores. Thus, the FAQ2 (with DK option) may be used to eliminate the usual practice effects found with FAQ1 repeated measures.

In a second study, 22 students were given both quizzes on the first and last day of an aging course. Both quizzes revealed a significant increase in percentage correct and decrease in anti-aging bias from time 1 to 2. Analysis indicates that if only the alternate forms were used, the same gain in knowledge would show, but there would be no significant change in bias found.

Coe, R., Miller, D., Prendergast, J., & Grossberg, G. (1982). Faculty resources for teaching geriatric medicine. *Journal of American Geriatrics Society, 30*, 63–66.

Self-administered questionnaires were sent to all faculty and staff members of the departments of internal medicine and psychiatry at the St. Louis University School of Medicine. The questionnaires asked for information about personal characteristics, practice characteristics, and interest in teaching geriatrics. Included were the FAQ1 and a measure of attitude from prescribed treatments for hypothetical patients differing only in age. Completed questionnaires were returned by 116 faculty members (25%). Results indicate that 40% wanted no involvement in teaching geriatrics. Of the remainder, most preferred a consultant's role on a clinical service. Despite extensive experience with elderly patients, respondents showed modest scores on knowledge (mean percentage correct on the FAQ1 was 67%), but there was little stereotyping of elderly patients. The mean percentage incorrect on the items indicating negative stereotyping was 30%. The responses to prescribed treatments for hypothetical patients differing in only age indicated less than 20% would have treated the elderly patient less aggressively than the younger patient. Implications for establishing a training program in geriatrics are discussed.

Cole, D., & Dancer, J. (1996). Comparison of four health care disciplines on the Facts on Aging and Mental Health Quiz. *Psychological Reports, 79*, 350.

Two hundred audiologists, speech-language pathologists, occupational therapists, and physical therapists were mailed the FAQMH to assess their knowledge in these areas. Results from the 104 returned surveys show that all groups scored means above 70% correct, indicating considerable knowledge which would help in their provision of services to older adults.

Courtenay, B., & Weidemann, C. (1985). The effects of a DK response on Palmore's Facts on Aging Quizzes. *The Gerontologist, 25*, 177–181.

Four groups of undergraduate students (total $N = 141$) completed one of four versions of Palmore's FAQs, in a test of the effects of a DK answer. The four versions were FAQ1, with and without a DK response, and FAQ2, with and without a DK response.

Results show that the DK response does decrease guessing, which decreases the percentage of errors from 33% to 30% on FAQ1 and from 45% to 33% on FAQ2. Conversely, the percentage correct was also reduced, from 67% to 54% on FAQ 1 and from 55% to 54% on FAQ2. Thus, the effects of a DK response were to reduce both correct and incorrect guesses on FAQ 1, but to reduce mainly incorrect guesses on FAQ2.

The effect on the anti-aged bias was minimal in FAQ1, but the scores were substantially reduced in FAQ2 (from 52% to 40%). However, the effect on the pro-aged bias was substantial in both the FAQ1 (from 38% to 31%) and the FAQ2 (from 38% to 23%). The net effects were to reduce the aged net bias score on FAQ1 from 10 to 4, but to increase this score from –14 to –17 on the FAQ2. Using a DK response also substantially improves internal reliability scores (Cronbach's alpha) from .30 to .60 on FAQ1 and from .16 to .52 on FAQ2.

Dail, P., & Johnson, J. (1985). Measuring change in undergraduate students' perception about aging. *Gerontology and Geriatric Education, 5*, 4.

Measurement of the effects of receiving information about aging was carried out with a group of 61 undergraduate students enrolled in a class on human development from middle childhood through old age. A comparison group consisted of 61 undergraduate students in a child development class. The FAQ1 was administered before and after a 5-week period of instruction about the aging process. Students who received the information about aging became more accurate in their perceptions of the process (mean percentage correct increased significantly from 66% to 74%) compared with students in the child development class (means increased from 65% to 68%).

However, posttest scores in the human development group did not significantly correlate with final exam. This was explained by the facts that the examination dealt with areas not covered by the FAQ1 and that the format of the examination (multiple choice and essay) was different from that of the FAQ1.

Dodson, M. (1990). The relationship between knowledge of and attitudes toward aging in an elderly population living in HUD-subsidized housing. *Dissertation Abstracts International, 51–08A*, 2618.

The FAQ1 (with DK option) was administered to 147 residents of U.S. Department of Housing and Urban Development (HUD) apartments for the elderly. The age range was 62 to 94 with a mean age of 78. The mean percentage correct answers was 53.

The correlation between knowledge of aging and positive attitudes ($r = .14$) was positive but not statistically significant. There was no significant difference in knowledge or attitude between older and younger residents, nor between more or less educated residents. The elders subscribed to the same common misconceptions about aging as those subscribed to by Palmore's (1977) younger subjects.

Doka, K. (1986). Adolescent attitudes and beliefs toward aging and the elderly. *International Journal of Aging and Human Development, 22*, 173–187.

This article reports the results of an oral history project that used adolescents to interview elderly informants. There were 24 students aged 12 to 16 in the oral history program and a control group of similar age and size. The oral history program was designed to maximize association with the elderly and appreciation for them as a living source of local history. The participants attended two all-day training sessions. The FAQ1 was administered before and after the project.

Both the experimental and control groups had considerable misinformation about aging and the elderly. On the pretest the mean score was 52% correct. The majority believed aged drivers have more accidents than younger drivers, that older workers are not as efficient as younger workers, and that older people cannot learn something new. They also overestimated the extent to which the elderly are isolated, lonely, angry, institutionalized, and poor.

There were no significant effects of the oral history project on knowledge or attitudes.

Donnelly, M., Duthie, E. Kirsling, R., & Gambert, S. (1987). The use of the combined Palmore and Dye and Sassenrath aging quizzes to assess gerontological knowledge in medical education. *Gerontology & Geriatrics Education, 6*, 11–24.

The utility of two easily administered tests, the FAQ1 and the Dye and Sassenrath (1979) scale, was examined using a pretest-posttest format with preclinical second-year medical students (*N* = 94) and a combined group of fourth-year medical students and internal medicine residents (*N* = 45) over a 3-year period. Test results were analyzed between subject groups, the two instruments, and by subject area. Both instruments were able to measure change (i.e., improvement). The FAQ1 mean score increased from 72% to 78% correct, and the Dye and Sassenrath (D & S) scale increased from 77% to 81%, both significant at the .05 level. The increases were also significant for two of the subject areas: biomedical and psychological. The sociodemographic area also increased (from 59% to 67%), but this was not statistically significant.

The second- and fourth-year students/residents performed at similar levels, although the fourth-year students found the sociodemographic items particularly difficult. Conversely, they found the psychological items less difficult than the second-year students, and they also gained more than the others from pretest to posttest. This is probably because the fourth-year students participated in a 1-month rotation, whereas the second-year students had only eight hours of instruction. However, correlations between pretest and posttest scores were high, and item difficulty remained fairly similar. This calls into question the educational significance of the gains in test scores. The authors conclude that, although these instruments measure knowledge gain in a pretest-posttest format, better designed instruments should be developed for the setting of medical education.

Dowd, S. (1983). Radiographers' knowledge of aging. *Radiological Technology, 54*,192–196.

The FAQ1 was given to a survey group of radiographers and students in Illinois. As a group, radiographers were found to be as well educated as any other group of health care professionals. A progression was seen from first-year students (60% correct) to second-year students (64%) to graduate radiographers (65%), in terms of knowledge of aging. The conclusion is reached that early clinical experience is responsible for this increase in knowledge about aging.

The most frequent misconceptions (with over 50% wrong) were Items 7, 12, 16, 19, 21, and 24.

Dudley, K. (1992). *A study of the relationship between death anxiety and negative bias toward the elderly among counselors*. M.S. thesis, Division of Counseling Psychology, University of Oregon.

Seventy-six counselors returned questionnaires including the FAQ1, FAQ2, and FAMHQ. There was no significant relationship between death anxiety and negative bias toward the elderly; however, there was a significant correlation (r = .41) between the FAQ1 and death anxiety, and a stronger correlation (r = .65) between the FAQ2 and death anxiety. There was a high correlation (r = .91) between scores on the two FAQs. The sample had significantly lower knowledge of aging and the elderly than other professional groups. There were no significant differences between gender or age groups in their mean scores on the FAQs.

Duerson, M., Thomas, J., Chang, J., & Stevens, C. (1992). Medical students' knowledge and misconception about aging: Responses to Palmore's FAQ's. *The Gerontologist, 32*, 171–174.

The FAQ1, FAQ2, & FAMHQ (with DK option) were administered as a single test to third-year medical students before and after their 6-week Community Health and Family Medicine clerkship. The clerkship contributed to a small improvement in students' knowledge about the aged, net bias scores decreased from pretest to posttest, there was no significant difference between male and female students, and scores on FAQ1 were significantly higher than scores on FAQ2 both pretest and posttest.

Durand, R., Roff, L., & Klemmack, D. (1981). Cognitive differentiation and the perception of older persons. *Research on Aging, 3*, 333–344.

Using data collected from a probability sample of 1,012 adults in Alabama, this study examines the relationships among knowledge about aging, negative net bias in knowledge about aging, fear about the consequences of being old, and differentiation of image of older persons. Cognitive differentiation was measured by having subjects evaluate 15 bipolar adjective pairs describing older persons in general, selected from Rosencranz and McNevin's (1969) multifactorial measure of image. Differentiation was operationalized by computing the variance of the responses across all 15 items. Knowledge about aging was measured by the FAQ 1. Net bias about aging was based on the difference between the number of incorrect answers to the 16 negative- and 5 positive-bias questions. Fear about the consequences of being old was measured by a four-item index developed for this study.

Those who were more knowledgeable about aging had lower negative bias scores ($r = -.26$) and less fear of the consequences of being old ($r = -.22$). Also, those with more knowledge about aging had a less differentiated image of older persons ($r = -.15$). Third, those who had more negative bias and those with more fear about the consequences of being old had more complex images of older persons ($r = -.19$ and .18, respectively).

These findings support the vigilance hypothesis as applied to the image of older persons: Those who are unfamiliar with and dislike older persons will be more vigilant about them and develop more differentiated images about them.

Duthie, E., & Gambert, S. (1983). The impact of a geriatric medicine rotation on internal medicine resident knowledge of aging. *Gerontology & Geriatric Education, 3*, 233–236.

The FAQ1 and a 40-item quiz on knowledge of geriatrics (Dye & Sassenrath, 1979) were used prior to and after a rotation in geriatrics for residents at the Medical College of Wisconsin. Scores were analyzed for the nine residents who cooperated. The items were divided into three subject areas: biomedical, psychiatric, and social.

The total mean score was 70% correct on the FAQ 1. This is the same score reported by Holtzman and Beck (1981) from undergraduate medical students. This suggests that merely being exposed to the elderly while in training does not lead to acquisition of knowledge in itself.

Significant improvement was noted, following the geriatric rotation, on the psychiatric items from the FAQ1 and on the biomedical and psychiatric items when questions from both quizzes were grouped. No significant improvement was noted on the social items from the FAQ1.

Eaglestein, A., & Weinsberg, E. (1985). *Knowledge and attitudes of teenagers concerning the elderly.* Discussion papers produced by the Joint Israel Brookdale Institute of Gerontology and Adult Human Development in Jerusalem.

The FAQ1 was translated into Hebrew and administered to 173 10th grade students (mean age: 17 years). The mean percentage correct was 56. The mean positive bias score was 22%, and the mean negative bias score was 50%. There were no significant correlations between demographic variables and the percentage correct nor positive and negative bias scores. However, there were significant positive correlations between the semantic differential scores (a measure of positive attitude) and knowledge as well as with the positive bias score.

Eakes, G. (1986). *The relationship between death anxiety and attitudes toward the elderly among nursing staff.* Unpublished manuscript.

Questionnaires were returned by 159 nurses in six nursing homes. Death anxiety was measured by Templer's (1977) scale, and negative attitude toward the elderly was measured by the anti-aged bias score on the FAQ1.

Nurses with high levels of death anxiety had significantly more negative attitudes toward the elderly than those with low levels. Also, there was a significant relationship ($r = .21$) between death anxiety and negative attitudes. However, there were no significant differences in death anxiety or attitudes by subject's age, race, length of experience, staff position, experience in witnessing a death, recent experience of death of someone close, amount of contact with death, religious faith, strength of religious beliefs, or participation in a course on the elderly or death and dying.

Eckel, F. (1977). *Knowledge about aging among pharmacy students.* Unpublished table.

The FAQ1 was given to 132 pharmacy students at Duke University. The mean score was 61% correct, and the range was from 40% to 88%.

Edwards, M., & Aldous, I. (1996). Attitudes toward and knowledge about elderly people: A comparative analysis of students of medicine, English and computer science and their teachers. *Medical Education, 30*, 221–225.

Attitudes toward and knowledge about elderly people were assessed in 1,091 students and lecturers from the London Hospital Medical College and the English and Computer Science departments of Queen Mary and Westfield College, London. Knowledge about the elderly was measured by the FAQ1. Attitudes were measured by the Rosencranz and McNevin Semantic Differential scale. A higher level of knowledge about elderly people was found both in medical students and in medical lecturers compared with their counterparts in the English and Computer Science departments. The cross-sectional data indicated that medical students developed a significantly increasing knowledge about elderly people as they progressed through their training, in contrast to students of English and Computer Science. A significant correlation was found between high levels of knowledge about elderly people, and positive attitudes toward them.

Edwards, R., Plant, M. Novak, D., Beall, C., & Baumhover, L. (1992). Knowledge about aging and Alzheimer's disease among baccalaureate nursing students. *Journal of Nursing Education, 31*, 125–127.

The FAQ2 was used to measure nursing students' knowledge of aging, and the Alzheimer's Disease Knowledge (ADK) test developed by Dieckmann et al. (1988). Knowledge of aging was not found to be related to scores on the ADK. The students as a group exhibited a negative bias toward the elderly as measured by the FAQ2.

Ellor, J., & Altield, S. (1980, November). *Knowledge and attitudes of hospital personnel toward elderly patients*. Paper presented at the annual meeting of the Gerontological Society of America, San Diego.

This study examines the correlates of knowledge about aging and attitudes toward working with the elderly and their families among hospital personnel with patient contact. The FAQ 1 and the Ellor Altfeld Attitudes Scale were administered to staff members at two community hospitals (Hospital A: $N = 324$; Hospital B: $N = 119$).

The mean percentages correct for each of the samples were lower than those reported by Palmore (1977) for undergraduate students

(Hospital A = 62%; Hospital B = 60%). Scores on the quiz were not related to staff's age, sex, or number of years of education.

Further analysis of the data revealed (a) no relationship between knowledge and age, profession, education, or length of professional experience; (b) no statistically significant correlations between attitude and any of the demographic variables, with the exception of a mild positive correlation between age and attitude; and (c) no statistically significant correlations between knowledge and attitude toward the elderly.

Subsequent use of these instruments by three independent researchers has supported these findings, thus challenging the commonly held assumption that factual knowledge about aging leads to improved attitudes toward the elderly and subsequently improves the quality of care given to older persons.

Ellison, J. (1991). A study of corporate managers' knowledge regarding age and ability of the older worker. *Dissertation Abstracts International, 52–11A*, 4101.

The FAQ and "An Overview of Older Workers" were used in acquiring data from 165 corporate managers on their knowledge. It was found that the managers' knowledge was less than that of members of a chapter for the American Association of Retired Persons. Changes should be made before "An Overview of Older Workers" is used in additional research.

Eyster, C. (1979, January 28). *Knowledge about aging among high school students*. Unpublished letter to E. Palmore.

The FAQ1 was given to a random sample of 100 high school students in a private school in Washington, DC. Sixty-four students responded. The mean score was 60% correct with a range of 32% to 84%. The most frequent misconceptions were reflected in items 7, 16, 19, and 24.

Filipcic, S. (1990). *Nursing home nurses' knowledge regarding the facts on aging*. Master's thesis, Department of Physiological Nursing, University of Washington, Seattle.

The FAQ1 (with DK option) was administered to 41 registered and licensed practical nurses in three rural and metropolitan-area nursing homes in western Washington. The mean score correct was 16.7 (67%). Attendance at continuing education courses related to the elderly was found to be associated with higher scores. Knowledge of aging was determined to be insufficient to fulfill the expectations of the Standards of Gerontological Nursing Practice set down by the American Nurses' Association.

Francis, C. (1991). *Assessing knowledge and attitudes about the elderly in acute care hospital and nursing home registered staff nurses*. Unpublished abstract of a study in the Veterans Administration Medical Center, East Orange, NJ.

The FAQ1 and the Tuckman-Lorge Attitude Toward Old People Scale were administered to 39 acute care and nursing home nurses. Cronbach's alpha found a low score (.57) for internal reliability for the FAQ. However, both groups of nurses had mean scores with over half the items correct (acute care: 14; nursing home: 15). Knowledge and attitudes were not significantly different between the two groups.

Geboy, M. (1982). Use of the Facts on Aging Quiz in dental education. *Gerontology and Geriatrics Education, 3*, 65–67.

The FAQ 1 was used in the first lecture of a 6-hour geriatric and handicapped-patient unit in the dental curriculum. There were 59 student participants. Fewer than 10% of the students had taken a course in human development, aging, or death and dying. Students found the quiz interesting and stimulating. The average score-was 77% correct. The majority missed Items 7, 16, 17, 19, 21, 23, and 24. This is similar to the findings of Palmore (1977).

Gibson, J., Choi, Y., & Cook, D. (1993). Service providers' knowledge and misconceptions about old age. *Educational Gerontology, 19*, 727–741.

Two hundred forty-five service providers in five settings were tested with the FAQ1. Findings: (a) Overall average score was 64% correct; (b) developments disabilities service providers scored lower than other service providers; and (c) the areas with the most misconceptions were psychological aspects of aging, demography, and socioeconomic status of aged.

Goulet, Y. (1982). *Faits concernant l'avance en age: Un bref quiz*. Unpublished translation of FAQ1.

This is a translation of the FAQ1 and its documentation, which were adapted to apply to Canada. A "?" response was added to represent "don't know."

Greenhill, E., & Baker, M. (1986). The effects of a well older adult clinical experience on students' knowledge and attitudes. *Journal of Nursing Education, 25*, 145–147.

This study was designed to test whether or not a planned learning experience with well older adults would exert a positive influence on nursing students' attitudes, on their level of gerontological knowledge, and on their willingness to work with older adults after graduation. Students in a baccalaureate program were divided into treatment or control groups, based on their attitudes on Kogan's Attitude Toward Old People Scale (1961). Knowledge was measured by the FAQ1. Half of the students were given experiences with well elderly, and the other group had no experience with this population. Differences in pretest and posttest scores were compared by analysis of variance.

All students, regardless of planned experience with older adults, increased their knowledge. Students who initially had negative attitudes significantly improved their attitudes, regardless of the type of clinical experience. The investigation failed to support the idea that experiences with well elderly would make a difference on attitude and knowledge base.

Greenslade, V. (1986). *Evaluation of postgraduate gerontological nursing education*. Unpublished manuscript.

This article compared two groups of Canadian nurses who worked with the elderly: 10 nurses who had completed the post–basic gerontological nursing program and 10 nurses who had not. The second group was matched to the first on age, experience, education, location, and work area. The FAQ1, with two items revised to refer to Canadian statistics and a DK response category, was used. The group with the gerontological program had significantly more correct answers (83%) than the other group (61%). The items on which there was a 30% or more difference in correct scores between the two groups were 7, 12, 19, and 24.

A second questionnaire was sent to coworkers, asking them whom they would consult for information about gerontology. The most frequently mentioned type of person was a coworker who had post–basic gerontological training.

A third questionnaire was sent to the nursing supervisors of each of the participants in the first group, asking about knowledge sharing among the participants. Over three fourths agreed that knowledge sharing was frequent among coworkers, clients, and families, and that this sharing increased after the program.

Groseck, J. (1989). A study of attitudes Philadelphians have toward old people, their knowledge about aging, and demographic characteristics. *Dissertation Abstracts International, 50–06A*, 1768.

The FAQ was used with 728 responses to a postal survey among a stratified random sampling of Philadelphians. Knowledge about aging and attitudes toward elders were related to life satisfaction. Mean scores on the FAQ suggest that Philadelphians are deficient in their knowledge about aging. Respondents moving up in the hierarchies of education, occupation, and income had increasing knowledge about aging accompanied by increasingly more negative attitudes toward old people. An exception to the pattern was the age criterion: increasing age of respondents was accompanied by increasing knowledge and more positive attitudes. Asian respondents had the least knowledge about aging and more negative attitudes toward the old. It was suggested that the low knowledge scores might relate to problems with the English language and to cultural differences in the meanings of words.

Haas, W., & Olson, P. (1983, November). Family physicians and geriatrics. Paper presented at the 1983 annual meeting of the Gerontological Society of America, San Francisco.

This paper reports on a comprehensive inventory of family physicians' knowledge and views of geriatrics. A self-administered survey including the FAQ1 and measures of geriatric attitudes and clinical knowledge was returned by 95 family physicians (response rate was 61%).

The doctors' knowledge of the general aging process was moderate: The mean score on the FAQ1 was 60% correct. No strong or significant associations were found to exist between the geriatric attitude indexes and the general or clinical knowledge scores. Geriatric education also was not related to general or clinical knowledge of aging. The doctors knew more about senescence than the social aspects of aging. Items missed by a majority were 7, 16, 17, 19, and 24.

Hannon, J. (1980). Effects of a course on aging in a graduate nursing curriculum. *Journal of Gerontological Nursing, 6*, 604–615.

The FAQ1 was used to evaluate the effects on 10 students of a course on aging in a graduate nursing curriculum. The course included written and oral reports by students, special projects, individual relationships with elderly persons, analysis of aging as portrayed in a work of fiction, and a written statement of their own beliefs and feelings about their own aging.

The mean score increased: 68% correct before the course to 78% correct afterward. Before the course all students were in error on the current percentage of aged in the United States. The majority had errors on Items 7, 16, 21, and 24. Also, Items 12, 15, and 22 showed an unexplainable increase in the percentage of errors. Students tended to have a negative net bias score both before and after the course, with no significant change in the bias score.

The Kogan (1961) Attitudes Toward Old People Scale was also used. After the course there tended to be more disagreement with negative items and more agreement with positive items; that is, attitudes became more favorable toward old people.

Harris, D., & Changas, P. (1994). Revision of Palmore's second Facts on Aging Quiz from a true-false to a multiple-choice format. *Educational Gerontology, 20*, 741–754.

The multiple-choice version was administered to 195 introductory sociology students, and the standard true-false version was given to a second group of 180 introductory sociology students. Compared with the true-false version, the multiple-choice version (a) showed a substantial decrease in guessing and thus increased the likelihood that a score was an accurate reflection of a respondent's knowledge, (b) had greater internal consistency and reliability, (c) showed a trend toward higher discriminatory power, and (d) identified more specifically some misconceptions about aging. (See Chapter 2.)

Harris, D., Changas, P., & Palmore, E. (1996). Palmore's first Facts on Aging Quiz in a multiple-choice format. *Educational Gerontology, 22*, 575–589.

A multiple-choice version and a true-false version of Palmore's first Facts on Aging Quiz were tested on a sample of 501 college students. The multiple-choice version reduced the chances of guessing the correct answer and reduced measurement error for average and above-average respondents. (See Chapter 1.)

Harris, N. (1979). *Secondary-school home economics teachers' attitudes toward the aged and knowledge of aging.* Unpublished manuscript from College of Home Economics, Florida State University, Tallahassee.

Knowledge about and attitudes toward aging in a random sample of all secondary-school home economics teachers in Florida were investigated. A total of 140 teachers completed a 10-page demographic information questionnaire, the FAQ1, and the Tuckman-Lorge Scale (1952) (to determine attitudes toward the aged).

The Kuder-Richardson statistic was used to establish reliability of the instruments. The Tuckman-Lorge Scale was found reliable, but reliability of the FAQ1 was found to be questionable.

Scores on both instruments were generally low. Scores did not vary significantly according to age or amount of formal education about aging. Scores on the two scales were related, and scores on the FAQ1 could be used to predict scores on the Tuckman-Lorge Scale.

It was concluded that preservice and in-service gerontological training programs should be provided for secondary-school home economics teachers.

Holtzman, J., & Beck, J. (1979). Palmore's Facts on Aging Quiz: A reappraisal. *The Gerontologist, 19*, 116–120.

The FAQ1 was reconsidered in light of the results of over 500 administrations to health workers and to health occupation students at the Southern Illinois University School of Medicine and the University of Iowa College of Dentistry. The questionnaire also included Rosencranz and McNevin's (1969) Aging Semantic Differential.

In terms of the four purposes proposed by Palmore (1977), the quiz was found to be a useful tool for stimulating group discussions; there were no significant differences in total scores between sexes or ages, but better educated groups tended to get more correct; similar myths tended to prevail among members of the different occupational groups (Kendall's coefficient of concordance = .85); however, there was only a weak correlation (r = –.27) between the aged net bias scores and the Semantic Differential scores, which indicates that the FAQ1 is not an accurate measure of attitudes toward the aged. This last conclusion is contrary to Klemmack's (1978) assertions that the test actually measures bias rather than knowledge. It was concluded that the $_F$AQ1 has utility for three of the four purposes proposed by Palmore.

Holtzman, J., & Beck, J. (1981). Cognitive knowledge and attitudes toward the aged of dental and medical students. *Educational Gerontology, 6*, 195–207.

This study examines the attitudes and knowledge of over 283 dental and medical students at different stages in their professional education, using Rosencranz and McNevin's Semantic Differential and the FAQ1.

The mean knowledge score for all students was 65% correct, with medical students scoring significantly higher than dental students (70% compared with 64%). There were no significant differences by sex. The third-year medical students, who had taken a required geriatrics course, scored significantly higher (75%) than any other group. They also had a positive net bias score (+1.9), compared with the other groups, all of whom had negative net bias scores (from –7.5 to –14.8). An analysis of covariance confirms this difference.

There was a moderate and significant direct relationship between overall attitude (Semantic Differential) scores and knowledge scores (r = .26). It was concluded that increased knowledge of aging has only a modest effect on improving attitudes toward the aged.

Holtzman, J., Toewe, C., & Beck, J. (1979). Specialty preference and attitudes toward the aged. *The Journal of Family Practice, 9*, 667–672.

The relationship between the attitudes and knowledge regarding the aged and specialty preference of undergraduate medical students (N = 314) at three medical schools was studied. The FAQ1 and the Rosencranz and McNevin Aging Semantic Differential were used.

No significant differences in attitudes were found between students classified by class (freshman, sophomore, etc.) or by sex. A significant though weak relationship ($r = .27$) between class and level of knowledge was found (higher classes had more knowledge). Students indicating a preference for family practice were not significantly different in knowledge from all other students (mean score = 69% correct). However, when all students expressing a preference for a primary-care specialty were combined, their mean scores showed more positive attitudes toward the aged than their peers. Knowledge of aging did not differ significantly between these groups.

Huckstadt, A. (1983). Do nurses know enough about gerontology? *Journal of Gerontological Nursing, 9*, 392–396.

This study is based on 252 usable questionnaires returned by registered nurses in Kansas. Knowledge was measured by the FAQ1. There were 21 independent variables.

The total mean score was 61.5% correct. The items with more than 59% of responses incorrect were 7, 8, 16, 17, 19, 23, 24, and 25. Of the 21 independent variables, only level of further education after basic nursing preparation had a significant relationship to knowledge about aging.

Iannone, J. (1986). *Relationship between long-term care nurses' attitude toward the elderly and their knowledge of gerontological nursing, age, number of years in long-term care nursing, and level of nursing preparation*. Unpublished manuscript.

The purpose of this study was to investigate the relationship between the level of gerontological nursing knowledge and attitudes toward the elderly of registered nurses in long-term care. Selected demographic factors were also examined to determine if age, number of years employed in caring for the elderly, and level of nursing education influence a nurse's attitudes toward the elderly. The FAQ1 and Kogan's (1961) Attitudes Toward Old People Scale were used. The mean score on the FAQ1 was 60% correct. There was a small but significant positive correlation between nurses' knowledge of gerontological nursing and their attitudes toward the elderly ($r = .21$). However, there were no significant relationships between nurses' attitudes toward the elderly and the other variables.

Jeffrey, D. (1978, February 13). Knowledge about aging among undergraduates and graduate students. Unpublished letter to E. Palmore.

The FAQ1 was administered to 21 undergraduate students and to 30 graduate students studying gerontology. The mean scores were 60% correct for the undergraduates and 81% for the graduate students. This demonstrates the effects of the graduate study in gerontology.

Jones, V. (1993). *Attitudes and knowledge level of nursing personnel toward elderly persons.* Master's thesis at Russell Sage College, Troy, NY.

The FAQ1 was administered to 23 nursing personnel in an acute care setting with clients mostly over age 65 (Group I), and to 20 nurses in a long-term care setting (Group II). Both groups had knowledge levels equal to college and graduate/gerontology students. There were moderate relationships between knowledge and attitudes for Group I ($r = .35$) and II ($r = .66$).

Kabacoff, R., Shaw, I., Putnam, E., & Klein, H. (1983). Comparison of administrators and direct service workers in agencies dealing with the elderly. *Psychological Reports, 52*, 979–985.

This paper presents comparative information, gained from mailed questionnaires, on the attitudes, knowledge, and perceptions of clients' needs held by 62 administrators and 57 direct-service personnel workers with the aged. The FAQ1 and Kogan's (1961) Attitudes Toward Old People Scale were used. There were no significant differences on the FAQ1 between the administrators (mean score = 70% correct) and the direct-service workers (mean score = 68% correct). Also, there were no significant differences by age, sex, or years of experience. However, there was a significant educational effect: Those with graduate education had a mean score of 75% correct, those with bachelor's degrees had 68% correct, and those with no college degrees had 61% correct.

The administrators and direct-service workers were remarkably similar on all dimensions.

Kahana, E., & Kiyak, H. (1984). Attitudes and behavior of staff in facilities for the aged. *Research on Aging, 6*, 395–416.

In an attempt to examine the relationship between staff attitudes and behavior toward elderly, 72 staff members from nursing homes who had completed attitude questionnaires were observed and their behaviors recorded on a behavioral observation checklist. Positive and negative stereotyping was measured by the subscales of the FAQ1. The evaluative attitudes were assessed with a modified version of the Rosencranz and McNevin (1969) scale. Behavioral intentions toward the elderly were measured by responses to two hypothetical problems. There were two subscales developed: tendency to encourage dependency and tendency to encourage independence. Behaviors were also observed.

There were moderate but significant correlations between behavioral intentions and stereotypes: The more stereotypes staff members held (positive or negative), the less likely they were to favor independence and the more likely they were to encourage dependence.

In a multiple regression analysis of the predictors of positive parenting toward aged clients, positive stereotypes were the most significant predictors but in a negative direction; that is, the more positive stereotypes held, the less likely staff members were to display positive parenting. Tendency toward negative stereotyping had little effect on behavior. Positive stereotyping was also the most significant predictor of positive affection toward aged clients but, again, in a negative direction: Those with more positive stereotypes were less likely to express positive affect.

Keller, M. (1986). *Misconceptions about aging among nurses*. Unpublished manuscript.

The FAQ1 was administered to four groups (N = 267): staff of the Chronic Disease Branch, NC, Division of Health Services; nurses in 10 NC nursing homes; staff of the NC Division on Aging and Area Agencies on Aging; and nurses in local health departments.

The combined groups had a mean anti-aged bias score of 61% and a mean pro-aged bias score of 36%, resulting in a net bias score of –25. The nurses in the nursing homes and the local health departments had substantially higher anti-aged bias scores than average (74% and 67%, respectively). The highest error rate occurred in Items 7, 16, 17; 19, 21, 23, and 24.

King, P., & Cobb, M. (1983). Learning to care. *Journal of Gerontological Nursing, 9*, 289–392.

This study describes changes in the knowledge about aging of nursing students following an 11-week rotation with the aged. The FAQ1 was used to measure knowledge among 46 students.

Over 70% of the students had misconceptions about Items 7, 16, 22, 23, and 24 before the rotation. Following the rotation, there was a reduction in the first three misconceptions but not the last two. The net bias score decreased slightly (from –8 to –6) after the rotation. The total mean number correct increased slightly (from 16 to 17) after the rotation. Seventeen of the 25 items showed a reduction in errors after the rotation.

Klemmack, D. (1978). An examination of Palmore's FAQ. *The Gerontologist, 18*, 403–406.

The FAQ1 was used to examine level of information on aging among a stratified, random sample of 202 adults residing in a midsized southern city.

It was found that the discriminatory power of the seven items with highest or lowest scores was below usual standards for tests. Also, item-to-total-score correlation coefficients were not statistically significant for 18 of the items and, of the remaining seven items, only four had the predicted positive relationship. Consequently, the author thought there was little reason to believe that the total score on the FAQ is reflective of an individual's level of information on aging.

However, a factor analysis suggested that the FAQ1 does measure the degree to which respondents subscribe to a negative image of older persons. Most of the items designated by Palmore as reflecting positive or negative bias show the expected loadings on the First Principle Factor. (See Palmore, 1978.)

Klemmack, D., & Roff, L. (1981). Predicting general and comparative support for government providing benefits to older persons. *The Gerontologist, 21*, 592–599.

This study examines general and comparative public support for the government providing benefits to older persons, using data gathered from a probability sample of 1,015 adult residents of Alabama. The measure of general support was a six-item index developed to measure attitudes toward government involvement in economic provision for the elderly. It included statements such as, "Government should help older people by making sure that they have enough income to live comfortably," and "The government spends too much money on older people." Rank-order format, constant sum scales (Tull & Hawkins, 1976) were used to measure comparative public support for the government providing benefits to older persons: Respondents were given 100 points and asked to allocate them among 10 programs including "Benefits for older people like Medicare and Social Security." Another constant sum scale was used for 10 eligibility criteria including "60 or older." There were four attitude-toward-older-persons variables: Palmore's FAQ1, the net bias score, an abbreviated version of Rosencranz and McNevin's (1969) image of older persons scale, and a personal anxiety about being older scale.

Support for the government providing benefits to older persons was extremely high: Only 6% thought that the government spends too much money on older people. Benefits for older persons ranked second only to national defense among the list of 10 possible uses of tax dollars. Respondents also would have had the government allocate more funds to programs for which attaining 60 is the sole eligibility criterion than to programs for people in the other nine eligibility groups.

Correlates of general support for the government providing benefits to older persons were dominated by support for welfare and concern for the personal consequences of being old. Correlates of comparative support for older persons included having less education, being eligible for government benefits of any kind, being younger, and being in good health. Knowledge about aging was not significantly correlated with type of support.

Klemmack, D., & Roff, L. (1983). Stimulus evaluation and the relationship between a deterministic cognitive system and cognitive differentiation. *The Journal of Psychology, 113*, 199–209.

Using data gathered from a probability sample of 1,015 adult residents of Alabama, this study examined the relationships among personality traits associated with a deterministic cognitive system, fear of aging, negative stereotyping of older persons, and cognitive differentiation in the domain of "old person." The latter was measured by computing the variance in responses to 15 bipolar adjective pairs (from Rosencranz & McNevin, 1969). Negative stereotyping was measured by Palmore's net bias score on the FAQ1. Fear of aging was measured by a four-item Likert index.

Persons with a deterministic cognitive system tended to have cognitive differentiation in the domain of "old person." Stereotyping and fear of aging help explain this relationship: Persons with deterministic cognitive systems tend to have negative views of older people and, as predicted by the vigilance hypothesis, this makes them more vigilant about older persons, which develops a more differentiated picture of older persons.

Kline, D., Scialfa, C., Stier, D., & Babbitt, T. (1990). Effects of bias and educational experience on two knowledge of aging questionnaires. *Educational Gerontology, 16*, 297–310.

The preponderance of positive valenced items on the FAQ1 is such that scores on the test may be more representative of a respondent's attitude toward, than knowledge about aging, positive attitudes being associated with a higher FAQ score. In experiment 1, the FAQ's vulnerability to bias was tested by having young adults complete the FAQ under instructions to adopt either a positive or negative bias toward the elderly, their scores being compared with their own performance when requested to respond neutrally. Scores on the FAQ were found to be greatly affected by the direction of bias.

A new Knowledge of Aging and the Elderly (KAE) questionnaire, patterned after the FAQ, but balanced in item valence, was evaluated using the same procedure. The KAE was shown to be relatively immune to direction of bias. In experiment 2, a comparison of the FAQ and the KAE indicated that the KAE was also more sensitive to course-based differences in knowledge about aging. (See Palmore, 1990, for comment.)

Kline, T., & Kline, D. (1991a). The association between education, experience, and performance on two knowledge of aging and elderly questionnaires. *Educational Gerontology, 17*, 355–361.

Compared 42 students in gerontology courses (a) at the beginning and end of an academic term and (b) with nongerontology students on both the FAQ1 and the KAE. No performance changes were observed on either instrument as a result of either short-term experience of a gerontology course of long-term personal/professional experience of a more general character. Higher scores, however, were associated with long-term differences in education on both the FAQ and the KAE. Findings suggest that general work experience with the elderly cannot substitute for formal training in gerontology. Results emphasize the importance of a formal gerontology/geriatric curriculum for those who work with older persons.

Kline, T., & Kline, D. (1991b). Identification of response bias on two knowledge of aging questionnaires by use of randomization tests. *Gerontology & Geriatrics Education, 11*, 67–75.

Two hundred thirty undergraduates (aged 17–45 years) completed both the FAQ1 and the KAE (Kline et al., 1990). Subjects (Ss) with positive or negative biases toward the elderly were differentiated by their responses to items of positive and negative valence on both the FAQ and KAE. Negatively biased Ss had significantly lower overall knowledge scores on the FAQ than those with a positive bias, but no such difference was observed on the KAE. The susceptibility of the FAQ to bias suggests that the KAE would be preferred when assessing gerontological knowledge without the confound of bias.

Knox, V., Gekoski, W., & Johnson, E. (1986). Contact with and perceptions of the elderly. *The Gerontologist, 26*, 309–313.

The equivocal relationship between contact with and perceptions of the elderly obtained in previous research is attributed to limitations in the way contact has been assessed. A 57-item questionnaire tapping a wide variety of aspects of contact, a three-dimension measure of attitudes toward and perceptions of the elderly, and Miller and Dodder's (1980) revision of the FAQ1 were administered to 110 undergraduates. Multiple regression analyses identified several aspects of quality of contact with the elderly that reliably predicted attitudes toward and perceptions of them.

However, general knowledge of aging (the FAQ1) was related only modestly to aspects of contact. Only one of the 57 dimensions of contact was significantly related to the FAQ1, and it explained only 6% of the variance. It appears that contact with the elderly has the greatest influence on one's pro or con views of old people and the least influence on knowledge about aging.

Koyano, W., Inoue, K., & Shibata, H. (1987). Negative misconceptions about aging in Japanese adults. *Journal of Cross–Cultural Gerontology, 2*, 131–137.

Knowledge about old age in 555 Japanese urban adults aged 30 to 59 years was measured by the FAQ1. The total mean score correct was 14.3 (57%). Educational background significantly related to level of knowledge. However, age, sex, and coresidence with elderly parents were not related to knowledge. Comparisons of percent positive errors and percent negative errors revealed that negative misconceptions about old age are commonly held by Japanese adults.

Kwan, A. (1982). *An examination of the validity of Palmore's Facts on Aging Quiz*. Unpublished abstract (Hong Kong). Available from E. Palmore.

The FAQ1 was examined as an indirect measure of age bias, using data gathered from a sample of 90 social work students at the University of British Columbia. The results suggest that the FAQ1 demonstrated low practical criterion and content validity for determining social work students' bias toward older persons. Although this instrument may have other uses, these data indicate that it is inadequate as a research tool in assessing age bias.

Laner, M. (1981). Palmore's FAQ: Does it measure learning? *Gerontology and Geriatrics Education, 2*, 3–7.

In the first study, 46 students in a social gerontology class were given the FAQ1 before and at the end of the course. The students were given the correct answers verbally after the first administration of the quiz, and there was free discussion about the answers. There was a comparison group of 43 students in another sociology class unrelated to gerontology, who were not given the correct answers. There was a significant increase in the social gerontology students' scores from a mean number correct of 16.7 to 21.7, but there was no increase in the comparison group's scores.

The second study was similar to the first, except the students were not given the correct answers to the quiz at any time. Again there was a significant increase among the social gerontology students (from 16.7 to 20.0) but not among the comparison students. It was concluded that the FAQ does measure learning about aging.

Levenson, R. (1978, January 19). *Effects of a course in psychology on knowledge about aging among undergraduate students*. Unpublished letter to E. Palmore.

Thirty undergraduate psychology students were administered the FAQ1 and the Kogan OP Scale (1961), before and after a course in psychology. The mean score was 61% correct before and 68% correct after the course, which was a significant increase. There was also a reduction in the anti-aged bias after the course (from 16.5% to 12.0%); however this change was not statistically significant. There was a significant correlation ($r = .31$) between the FAQ1 and the OP Scale in the first administration, so that students with more knowledge had more positive attitudes.

Levy, W., & West, H. (1985, October 19). *Knowledge of aging in human service professions*. Paper presented at the annual meeting of the Texas Chapter, National Association of Social Workers, Dallas.

The FAQ1 was administered to 164 community-dwelling older persons, to 140 ordained ministers, to 170 physicians, and to 155 social workers. The elderly had a mean score of 55% correct. There was no significant difference between scores of females and males, but the old-old (75–91 years) had a significantly better mean score (57%) than the young-old (52%). The most frequently missed items, in order of frequency missed, were 19, 23, 21, 24, 2, 7, and 16. The elderly had a negative net bias of –5. Males were more biased (–8) than females (–2), and the old-old were the most biased of all (–11). In comparison with the undergraduates reported by Palmore (1977), the elderly were significantly less knowledgeable but held similar misconceptions and were slightly less anti-aged.

The clergy had a mean score of 66% correct. There was no significant relationship between age and knowledge, nor between denomination and knowledge. The most frequently missed items, in order of frequency, were 19, 2, 24, 16, and 21. Clergy held high pro-aged bias, with a net bias score of +13. They knew more about aging than did the elderly, but the clergy's knowledge did not differ significantly from undergraduates'.

The physicians had a mean score of 68% correct, which is significantly better than the elderly and the undergraduates but is not significantly better than the clergy. Specialty subgroups had no significant differences in mean scores. The youngest cohort of physicians (30–39 years) scored significantly lower (65%) than the other cohorts. The most frequently missed items, in order of frequency, were 19, 23, 24, 16, and 7. The net bias score was slightly negative (–2).

The social workers had a mean score of 72% correct. This was significantly higher than any of the other groups in this study. Social workers in aging scored even higher: 86%. The most frequently missed items, in order of frequency, were 19, 24, 16, 21, and 12. Social workers had a very positive aged net bias of +10, but those in the field of aging had a negative net bias of −4

It appears there is a need for more education about aging, even among those who are elderly.

Levy, W., & West, H. (1989). Knowledge of aging among clergy. *Journal of Religion & Aging, 5*, 67–74.

The FAQ1 was administered to 140 ordained ministers representing Protestants, Catholics, and Jews. The mean percent correct was 66, and there was a pro-aged bias of 13%. Neither age nor denomination was significant in relation to knowledge.

Light, B. (1978, December 5). *Knowledge of aging among students, nurses, and residents of a nursing home*. Unpublished letter to E. Palmore.

Four groups were given the FAQ1: (a) undergraduate adult students taking a course in health statistics (*N* = 15), (b) professional and nonprofessional employees of a skilled nursing home (*N* = 15), (c) residents of a nursing home who had been there for 1 year or more (*N* = 6), and (d) graduate students in gerontology (*N* = 15). The employees in the nursing home had the highest average score (69% correct), followed by the graduate students in gerontology (66%), the aged in the nursing home (65%), and the undergraduate students (61%). The most frequently missed items (with less than 50% correct) were 2, 12, 16, 19, 21, and 24.

Linn, B., & Zeppa, B. (1987). Predicting third-year medical students' attitudes toward the elderly and treating the old. *Gerontology & Geriatrics Education, 7*, 167–175.

One hundred seventy-nine medical students were tested with the FAQ2 and the Osgood Semantic Differential and the Kogan Old Peoples scale. Greater knowledge as measured by the FAQ2 predicted more positive attitudes toward the elderly.

Linsk, N., & Pinkston, E. (1984). Training gerontological practitioners in home-based family intervention. *Educational Gerontology, 10*, 289–305.

Human service practitioners specializing in the elderly learned to maintain older persons at home using behavioral formats. A 15-hour training curriculum was taught in three formats: a continuing education institution, a 5-week class followed by consultation, and an in-service training program. The FAQ1 was included in the pretest and posttest assessments as a measure of knowledge.

There were significant improvements in knowledge of gerontology (from a score on the FAQ1 of 76% correct to 81% correct), of practice skills, and relevant behavioral principles. All three formats produced significant improvement with no significant differences between the formats.

Lusk, S., Williams, R., & Hsuing, S. (1990). An evaluation of the Facts on Aging Quizzes I & II. *Journal of Nursing Education, 34*, 317–324.

The FAQ1 and FAQ2 were administered to 63 freshmen nursing students. The correlation between scores on the two quizzes was low ($r = .04$) and alpha-coefficients (a measure of reliability) were low (.45 and .32). However, use of theta-coefficients (a less stringent measure of reliability) resulted in .60 and .64. The factors emerging in this study differed from Palmore's conceptual structure and explained only 45% of the variance. Results suggest that although the quizzes may be useful as a stimulus for discussion, revisions and testing need to be done if they are to be used for research purposes.

Luszcz, M. (1982). Facts on Aging: An Australian validation. *The Gerontologist, 22*, 369–372.

The FAQ1 was administered to 166 first- and third-year Australian undergraduates. After administration, documentation for the facts based on available Australian statistics was provided the students, and discussion was encouraged.

The quiz did stimulate lively group discussion, and students were particularly critical of some items (e.g., 20, 21, and 24). Some of the criticisms pertained to points raised by Miller and Dodder (1980) that dealt with choice of words, a preponderance of negative items, and subjectively based facts.

The third-year students scored 64% correct, whereas first-year students scored 58% correct. This may be related to the higher education of the third-year students or to the greater proportions of them who had worked with the elderly in nursing homes or through social welfare services. The most common misconceptions were on Items 7, 11, 16, 19, 20, 21, and 24. There is a fair degree of overlap in items missed by this sample and those quizzed by Palmore (1977). Student age had a small ($r = .21$) but significant correlation with quiz scores, but there was no significant difference between the sexes. The net bias scores were –19 for first-year and –17 for third-year students. These are more negative than the net bias scores in Palmore's sample.

Luszcz, M., & Fitzgerald, K. (1986). Understanding cohort differences in cross-generational, self, and peer perceptions. *Journal of Gerontology, 41*, 234–240.

Australian adolescents, middle-aged, and elderly people (30 per group) participated in a study exploring (a) their self-, intercohort, and intracohort perceptions; (b) ascribed social distance; (c) knowledge of aging; and (d) the relationships among these phenomena. Data were gathered using a Social Distance Scale, Goals of Life Index, FAQ1 (Miller & Dodder revision), and Aging Semantic Differentials. All participants were volunteers, living actively in typical middle-class communities.

In general, elderly adults were the most devalued, and middle-aged adults were the most favored cohort. Unfavorable attitudes toward elderly people were predicted more by age-related social distance and societally induced biases than differential investments in psychosocial life tasks. Appraising one's member cohort more favorably than those outside it was paralleled by a tendency to view the self more favorably than peers. The discrepancy between societal and older individuals' views of aging suggests that the "social breakdown syndrome" itself may be breaking down: Older adults are moving away from a characterization of themselves as ineffective and dependent.

Adolescents (60% correct on FAQ1) know less about aging than elderly adults (69%) know. The middle-aged group (67%) was not significantly different from either group. There was a high degree of consistency in the ordering of myths adhered to by the three groups.

Maeda, D. (1981). Multivariate analysis of knowledge about old people and the sense of responsibility toward parents, in the case of urban middle-aged persons. *Social Gerontology, 12*, 3–5.

The purpose of this article was to determine the most important factors that influence the knowledge level of and the attitude toward old people, as well as the sense of responsibility toward parents on the part of middle-aged men and women who are expected to provide support and care for aged parents. The sample ($N = 591$) was drawn from married men and women aged 20 to 49 and living in a residential area of Tokyo. The FAQ1 was used, and four scores were constructed to be used as dependent variables: knowledge, negative bias, general responsibility toward parent, and specific responsibility toward parent. Except for birth order (among men) and age, demographic and socioeconomic status variables were not significantly related to the knowledge level of and the attitude toward old people. In the case of women, negative relationship with respondent's mother in childhood was significantly associated with negative bias. Knowledge was not positively related to sense of responsibility toward parents, as was expected. On the contrary, among women, knowledge was negatively associated with general responsibility toward parents.

Massino, F. (1993). An analysis of variables related to students' attitudes toward and knowledge of elderly persons. *Dissertation Abstracts International, 54–05B*, 2809.

The sample included 91 doctoral candidates, 62 master's level gerontology students, and 108 undergraduates. Knowledge was measured by the FAQ and the Knowledge of Aging and Elderly Persons Questionnaire. Attitudes were assessed with the Aging Semantic Differential and the Aging Opinion Survey. Thirty-seven percent of the variance in knowledge of elderly persons was explained by level of education, number of courses taken, quality of contact with elderly, subjects' age, and a low preference rating for working with persons aged 0 to 17 years.

Matthews, A., Tindale, J., & Norris, J. (1984). The FAQ: A Canadian validation and cross-cultural comparison. *Canadian Journal on Aging, 3*, 165–175.

Describes the applicability of the FAQ1 in the Canadian context and provides documentation for quiz items. Potential problems of misinterpretation of items relating to the rate of institutionalization and income levels are noted. Undergraduate students had a mean score of 16.1 (64% correct), faculty had 18.4 (74% correct), and social gerontology students had 19.9 (80%). The usefulness of the quiz in identifying differences in knowledge levels in Canada is confirmed.

McCutcheon, L. (1986). Development of the Psychological Facts on Aging Quiz. *Community/Junior College Quarterly, 10*, 123–129.

The two forms of the FAQ have generally been found to be reliable, factual, and useful for calling attention to the many myths about aging. The advantage of a similar quiz that deals exclusively with psychological and sociological facts about aging is its greater relevance to courses in behavioral sciences. This study presented the Psychological Facts on Aging Quiz (PFAQ), based primarily on original and revised items from the FAQ.

Norms were presented for the PFAQ, based on community college students, and information about the derivation and difficulty of its items was presented. The mean score for 121 subjects was 13, and there was no significant differences in scores between the sexes and between older and younger students. The PFAQ was recommended for use in community college classes in the behavioral sciences.

McDowell, J. (1978). *Factors related to misconceptions about aging among nurses*. Unpublished manuscript.

A study was conducted to determine if years as a nurse, age, amount of continuing education in gerontology, gerontology in nursing school, level of nursing education, highest level of education, and percentage of caseload over age 65 were related to misconceptions and biases about the aged. The FAQ1 was administered to 169 nurses in home care and ambulatory care centers in a metropolitan area. The mean score was 72% correct. Seven statements were incorrectly answered by a majority of the nurses: 7, 11, 16, 19, 21, 23, and 24. They had a 31% anti-aged bias score and 51% pro-aged bias score, for a net bias score of +20.

The only independent variable significantly related to knowledge about aging was having a master's degree. There was a tendency for nurses with more hours of continuing education in gerontology to have higher scores, but this was not statistically significant. Nurses with baccalaureate or higher degrees also had significantly less negative bias toward the aged.

McKinlay, R. (1979a). *Knowledge about aging among graduate students in gerontology*. Unpublished tables.

The FAQ 1 was given to 31 graduate students in a gerontology workshop on "Historical Trends in Aging" at the University of Michigan, Ann Arbor, Michigan.

The mean score was 92% correct. This is one of the highest mean scores recorded for any group and indicates the effects of graduate education in gerontology on knowledge of aging.

McKinlay, R. (1979b). *Knowledge about aging among the aged*. Unpublished tables.

The FAQ 1 was given to five groups in Durham, NC, most of whom were over age 60: (a) ministers (N = 21), (b) Elderhostel participants (N = 43), (c) volunteers in the Retired Senior Volunteers Program (N = 12), (d) Durham residents over age 60 (N = 40), and (e) members of the Durham Senior Center board (N = 18).

The overall mean score was 64% correct. The members of the Senior Center board had the highest average score (73%), whereas the Durham residents over 60 had the lowest (59%). There were no significant differences by age group, sex, race, or marital status; however, those with a high school education or less had a mean score of 58% correct, while those with college education had a mean score of 69%. This indicates that the aged are as ignorant about aging as are younger persons, but that more education contributes to more knowledge about aging.

McMillon, G. (1993). Aging: Knowledge and attitudes of vocational home economics teachers. *Dissertation Abstracts International, 54–11A*, 4010.

The FAQ1 and the Semantic Differential scale were used to measure knowledge and attitudes toward aging of 307 teachers. Mean correct items were 60%. Scores indicate positive attitudes and above average knowledge (*Note:* 10% above chance).

Meiburg, A. (1981). *Knowledge of aging among clergy in Virginia.* Unpublished letter to E. Palmore.

The FAQ1 was administered to 22 clergy in Richmond, VA. Most of the clergy were affiliated with a hospital's chaplaincy service as volunteer helpers. The average correct score was 17.2 or 68%.

Miller, C. (1987). *Patterns of factual knowledge and misconceptions about aging revealed by family members of the elderly in a long term care facility.* Unpublished dissertation in the Department of Nursing, Mercy College, Yonkers, NY.

The FAQ1 was administered to 30 family members of elderly in a nursing home. About 40% or the responses were misconceptions. The family members closest in blood line, and those older than the residents had fewer misconceptions.

Miller, R., & Acuff, F. (1982). Stereotypes and retirement: A perspective from the Palmore FAQ. *Sociological Spectrum, 2*, 187–199.

This study focuses on the stereotypes that elderly retirees hold of old age and the socioeconomic and sociodemographic factors associated with these beliefs. The FAQ1 was administered to 224 retirees from a large corporation in the Southwest. The sample generally had above-average socioeconomic characteristics.

The results indicate that this sample was less likely to have stereotypes concerning old age (62% correct) than were similar cohorts from earlier studies (55% correct; Klemmack, 1978), but this could be due to their above-average socioeconomic characteristics. However, the stereotypes they did hold tended to be more negative than those of earlier studies.

Socioeconomic and sociodemographic characteristics of the retirees accounted for only a small proportion of the variation in total score ($r^2 = 16$). The characteristic most strongly associated with the total score was desire to work ($b = -.37$): Those desiring to work had fewer correct (more stereotypes). The characteristics explained somewhat more of the variation in positive and negative subscales ($r^2 = .25$ and .27). The characteristic most strongly associated with the positive subscale was perceived overall health ($b = +.37$): Those with better health had fewer positive stereotypes. The strongest characteristics associated with the negative subscale were desire to work ($b = +.28$) and income ($b = +.26$):

Those desiring to work and those with more income had more negative stereotypes.

Miller, R., & Dodder, R. (1980). A revision of Palmore's FAQ. *The Gerontologist, 20*, 673–679.

Because of theoretical problems with the Palmore FAQ, an alternative form of the scale was developed. These revisions correct the following problems: The ambiguous word "most" is replaced by "majority"; "double-barreled" statements containing two concepts are simplified to one concept; Item 13 is deleted because it is difficult to document; the poverty level is defined in absolute dollar values in Item 21; several items are reversed to even out the number of positive and negative bias items; and the subjective items clarify that they deal with self-reported feelings. They also suggest (but did not include) an optional DK response to the items.

The two forms were tested on a sample of 430 college students in introductory classes of a large southwestern university. Those who responded to the Miller-Dodder revision answered more items correctly (63%) than those who responded to the Palmore scale (58%). However, the use of "majority" compared with the use of "most" did not make a significant difference in how the questions were answered.

Similarly, defining the poverty level resulted in an increase of only 6% correct. The reversed items resulted in a 26% increase in correct responses on the reversed items. There was also considerable increase in correct responses on the subjective statements when the self-reporting was specified. Finally, "double-barreled" statements appeared to have influence on responses (see Palmore, 1981b).

Miller, R., & Dodder, R. (1984). An empirical analysis of Palmore's FAQ and the Miller-Dodder revision. *Sociological Spectrum, 4*, 53–69.

This article focuses on an empirical evaluation of Palmore's FAQ1 and the recent revision by Miller and Dodder (1980). The two measures were compared using similar samples of college students (total $N = 430$) at a large southwestern university. Contact with elderly persons, social distance from elderly, coursework in gerontology, experience working with elderly, and self-rated knowledge about the elderly were also assessed.

The total Palmore FAQ1 scores were not significantly correlated with any of the 13 other scales or subscales, but the Miller-Dodder revision was significantly correlated with four of these measures. However, the positive and negative subscales of Palmore's FAQ1 were correlated with most of the other measures in the expected directions, and 7 of the 26 correlations were significant. The Miller-Dodder revision subscales were similarly correlated with the other measures, but the correlations were less significant.

Items that dealt with subjective feelings of the elderly were analyzed separately from those that dealt with objective facts. Similarly, items that were reversed by Miller and Dodder and that were changed from "most" to "majority" were analyzed separately. The Miller and Dodder revisions of these subscales tended to show more significant correlations with the other measures than did the Palmore versions. It was concluded that, although the Miller-Dodder revision displayed somewhat stronger correlations with the other measures, neither the FAQ1 nor the Miller-Dodder revision correlated impressively with contact, attitudes, experience, or other measures of knowledge (see Palmore. 1981a).

Mishaan, M. (1992). The relationships among life satisfaction, level of activity, knowledge about aging, self-assessed health and perceived financial adequacy in a group of aged persons. *Dissertation Abstracts International, 53(1–A)*, 262

The FAQ1 was used to measure knowledge about aging in a group of aged persons in Brooklyn, NY. No significant relationship was found between life satisfaction and knowledge about aging, nor between level of activity and knowledge. Sex, age, income, and education were not significantly related to knowledge about aging.

Monk, A., & Kaye, L. (1982). Gerontological knowledge and attitudes of students of religion. *Educational Gerontology, 8*, 435–445.

This article reports on a study that examined the perceptions, experiences, and expectations of students of religion (*N* = 142) and their graduate counterparts (*N* = 216), by means of structured interviews. Rosencranz and McNevin's (1969) Aging Semantic Differential, the FAQ1, and original indices were used to operationalize the study variables.

Both groups had low gerontological knowledge scores: 62% correct for students and 63% correct for recent graduates. There tended to be more negative than positive bias toward the aged. There were significant positive correlations between knowledge and attitudes, ranging from $r = .17$ to $r = .26$. Also, more knowledge was significantly associated with desire to work with the aged and with an increase in the importance of the issue of old age for them.

Study findings lead to curricula development recommendations.

Murdaugh, J. (1978, February 5). *Knowledge of aging among geropsychiatric nurses*. Unpublished letter to E. Palmore.

Seven geropsychiatric nurses were administered the FAQ1. The mean score was 73% correct.

Murphy, R., Die, A., & Walker, J. (1986). Changing attitudes toward the elderly: The impact of three methods of attitude change. *Educational Gerontology, 12*, 241–251.

This article assesses the effectiveness of three different approaches in improving the attitudes of young people toward the elderly. Three groups of 21 undergraduate psychology students ages 17 to 25 participated in a workshop series of three single sessions presented in a different order to each group. The sessions consisted of an informational filmstrip dispelling myths about aging, an interview with an elderly man and woman selected for their nonstereotypical attitudes and behavior, and completion and discussion of the FAQ1. Kogan's (1961) Attitudes Toward Old People Scale with filler camouflage items, was administered to each group before the sessions, after the first session, and after the entire series. Kogan's Scale also was administered to a comparison group who did not participate in any of the workshop sessions.

Each experimental group showed a significant positive change in attitude over the comparison group after the first session, which indicated that each approach was effective. The largest change was experienced by the group who had direct contact with the elderly couple in the initial session, and their scores after the initial session were comparable with those of the other two treatment groups after all three sessions. Although the total workshop series was effective in changing attitudes toward the elderly, the pattern of change indicated that direct contact with the elderly couple was the principle factor in the workshop's success.

Netting, F., & Kennedy, L. (1985). Project RENEW: Development of a volunteer respite care program. *The Gerontologist, 25*, 573–583.

This article reports on the development and implementation of an in-home respite program using trained volunteers (*N* = 22) to provide at-home companionship and supervision for frail elderly persons while family members are absent. Project RENEW volunteers and families are described, and a discussion of difficulties and future directions is presented.

The FAQ1 and FAQ2 were administered to all volunteers prior to initial training sessions, to give the coordinator an idea of what knowledge volunteers had about aging. The range of scores on the two quizzes was between 56% and 85% correct, which suggests only a modicum of knowledge regarding the aging processes.

Noel, M., & Ames, B. (1989). Attitudes, knowledge, and problem-solving approach of Michigan dietitians about aging. *Journal of American Dietetic Association, 89*, 1753–1757.

Four instruments were used to survey active members of the American Dietetic Association in Michigan including the FAQ. Although dietitians' knowledge about aging generally was adequate, the questionnaire revealed that dietitians lacked knowledge in the areas of economic and health status; dietitians answered that older adults have a lower income and are sicker and more institutionalized than is, in fact, true.

Norris, J., Tindale, J., & Matthews, A. (1987). The factor structure of the FAQ. *The Gerontologist, 27*, 673–676.

The original FAQ1 was administered to three classes of undergraduate students in Family Studies courses at the University of Guelph, faculty in the same department, and three groups of public health nurses (*N* = 527).

The factors derived from responses to the FAQ1 were found to be different from those determined intuitively by Palmore. Also the reliability and validity of the scale was only moderate. However, the criterion-related validity was substantial; quiz scores and final grades for 15 students in a social gerontology course produced a significant positive relationship ($r = .45$). Also third-year social gerontology students scored significantly higher than others. It was recommended that the quiz be considered for only educational purposes and not for research. (See E. Palmore [1988] for comment.)

O'Hanlon, A., Camp, C., & Osofsky, H. (1993). Knowledge of and attitudes toward aging in young, middle aged, and older college students. *Educational Gerontology, 19*, 753–766.

The original FAQ1 and the Kline Knowledge of Aging and the Elderly scale were administered to 387 college students in New Orleans. The sample was divided into three age groups: young (mean = 20 years), middle-aged (mean = 38 years), and old (mean = 70 years). Knowledge scores were moderately related (r = .2 to .3) to either direct or indirect measure of attitudes, and scores on the knowledge tests were moderately related to each other (r = .25). In general, older subjects had higher knowledge scores (mean difference = 1 or 2 points) and more positive attitude scores (mean difference = 8%) than younger subjects. The age effect for knowledge remained after controlling for attitude.

Okuma, V., & Johnson, J. (1986). Use of gerontological knowledge in the elementary classroom. *Nursing Homes, 35*, 22–25.

Describes a unit on aging developed for use with gifted elementary school children in grades 1 to 5 in a Florida county. The unit was developed by an educator and a gerontological nurse in a long-term–care setting and was divided into three major areas: normal physiological effects of aging, psychosocial needs of the aged, and environmental needs. Specific teaching strategies were used to enhance the learning experience, such as simulations of sensory loss, watching a nationally known group of 70- to 90-year-old men playing softball, and visits to a nursing home and high-rise apartment complex for the elderly. The program was evaluated using a 10-item pretest-posttest format derived from the FAQ1 and by professional observations.

Scores showed a 23% mean improvement from pretest to posttest. The students' attitudes toward aging and the aged also were highly positive after completion of the unit, as indicated by written expressions of their feelings. Ways in which gerontological nurses can help to decrease negative attitudes toward aging in the community are suggested.

Palmore, E. (1977). Facts on aging: A short quiz. *The Gerontologist, 17*, 315–320.

This is the first publication of the FAQ1, its documentation, and results from studies using it at Duke University. The FAQ1 was designed to avoid the problems of the previous tests in that the FAQ1 is short, confined to factual statements that can be documented by empirical research, and covers the basic physical, mental, and social facts and the most common misconceptions about aging. The 25 true-false items are presented, the scoring key is given, and the items are documented and discussed.

The uses for the quiz include stimulating group discussion and clarification of misconceptions, measuring and comparing different groups' overall levels of information, identifying the most frequent misconceptions, indirectly measuring bias toward the aged, measuring the effects of lectures, and so forth. Undergraduate students in sociology classes ($N = 86$) had a mean score of 65% correct; 44 graduate students in aging and human development had a mean score of 80%; and faculty in aging and human development had a mean score of 90%. Items with 50% or more errors among the undergraduates were 7, 16, 19, 20, 21, 23, and 24.

Palmore, E. (1978). Professor Palmore responds. *The Gerontologist, 18*, 4–6.

This is a rebuttal of Klemmack's (1978) article. The criteria used in evaluating the quiz are inappropriate for the purposes specified, namely, measuring levels of information, identifying most frequent misconceptions, and measuring changes in information. The criteria of item discriminatory power and item-to-total correlation would be appropriate if the quiz were primarily psychometric in purpose, that is, if it were designed primarily to place a person relative to a normative group on a relatively stable and homogeneous trait (such as intelligence).

On the contrary, the quiz's purpose is primarily "edumetric": It is designed "to yield measurements that are directly interpretable in terms of specified performance standards." The specified performance standard in this case is the ability to distinguish between true and false statements about aging. Given this standard, it is irrelevant whether an item has high discriminatory power or has a high item-to-total correlation. Similarly, the fact that many of the items load heavily on a factor that could be called negative-positive image of aging has nothing to do with its validity as a measure of information on aging. An analogy would be a test of knowledge about state capitals consisting of 25 states with blanks for the capitals. The discriminatory power and item-to-total correlations of many of the items would be low, but this would be irrelevant to the validity of asking for the capitals of those states. Those students who got more state capitals correct know more about state capitals than do other students.

Palmore, E. (1980). The Facts on Aging Quiz: A review of findings. *The Gerontologist, 20*, 669–673.

This is a review of over 25 studies using the FAQ1. The most frequent misconceptions (with over half of the group guessing incorrectly) were Items 7, 11, 16, 19, 21, and 24. It was noted that five of these six misconceptions involve negative stereotypes of the aged.

The studies found little difference in mean FAQ1 scores between the sexes, races, or even between age groups when education is held constant. The one consistent demographic variable related to FAQ1 scores was education. More educated groups also were generally less biased against the aged; however, the validity of the FAQ1 as an indirect measure of bias is questioned because of low correlations with other measures of attitude toward the aged.

Before-and-after tests using the FAQ1 generally found substantial improvements in scores after training in gerontology. Group score reliability is high, and rank ordering in terms of difficulty of items is reliable, but item-to-total reliability is low because of several items that have unusually low item-to-total correlations. The validity of the FAQ1 as a measure of knowledge rests primarily on the face validity of the items and their documentation. Another support for the validity of the FAQ1 is the association between training in gerontology and higher FAQ1 scores.

Palmore, E. (1981a). The Facts on Aging Quiz: Part Two. *The Gerontologist, 21*, 431–437.

The FAQ2 is presented as an alternative form of the original Facts on Aging Quiz (FAQ1). Like the FAQ1, it consists of 25 true-false items. The test is presented, along with item documentation and the key to scoring. The test was developed primarily to be used in test-retest situations, to avoid the problem of practice effects when the first form is repeated on the retest. It can also be used for discussion and clarification of another 25 facts about aging.

There were nine frequent misconceptions (facts that over 50% did not know): 4, 6, 9, 10, 11, 12, 15, 20, and 24. Calculations of bias scores showed 48% negative bias, 29% positive bias, for a net bias score of –19.

When the FAQ2 is used as a retest for comparison with the FAQ1, it has been recommended that five points be added to the FAQ2 scores, to make them more equal to the FAQ1 because groups tend to get lower scores on the FAQ2. (This is not true, however, if a "don't know" option is used.)

The validity of the FAQ2 rests primarily on the statistics and studies in the documentation. Reliability between the two forms is satisfactory, based on correlations ranging from .50 to .80. However, interitem correlations tend to be low because the items represent many different dimensions of knowledge about aging.

Palmore, E. (1981b). Palmore responds. *The Gerontologist, 21*, 115–116.

This is a commentary on Miller and Dodder's (1980) revision of the FAQ1. Palmore agrees with five of the seven suggested changes, although the differences that these changes make appear to be trivial, according to Miller and Dodder's own study. Palmore agrees with the following changes: (a) Change "most" to "majority" in Items 3, 9, 11, 14, 15, and 20. (b) Change "double-barreled" statements to single concepts in Items 3, 11, and 17. However, the proposed change in Item 22 changes the meaning so that it is no longer true. The majority do not say they "would like to have some kind of work to do," simply because many already have some kind of work (including housework and volunteer work). The statement must include those who have some kind of work to be true. (c) Specify the poverty level in dollar amounts (item 24), but update this each year because the poverty level changes each year. (d) Change objective statements to subjective statements. This has already been incorporated in the 1980 revisions (Palmore, 1980). (e) Include DK as a possible response. This would be useful in distinguishing those who know they don't know and guess wrong, from those who think they know but do not know. (See Courtenay & Weidemann, 1985.)

We do not agree with two of the proposed changes: (a) Do not omit Item 13. It does discriminate between the few (9%) who think it is almost impossible for older persons to learn new things and the vast majority who know that it is not impossible for older persons to learn new things. The question of how long it takes them to learn is a different issue and is addressed by Item 12. (b) Most important, do not change five of the negative-bias items to positive-bias items. First, it is not necessary to do this because the formula for computing bias subtracts the percentage of negative-bias items wrong from the percentage of positive-bias items wrong, thus controlling for the number of each type. More important, the changes proposed are not the exact opposites of the original items. For example, although it is false that "the majority of old people say they feel miserable most of the time" (original Item 5), it is not true that the "the majority of older people say they are happy most of the time" (proposed revision). The majority would say they are somewhere in between miserable and happy most of the time. Thus, this revised item should be scored as false rather than true as assumed by Miller and Dodder. This kind of shift in meaning probably accounts for the large shifts in proportions getting the items "wrong."

Thus, some of the proposed revisions would slightly improve the FAQ1, but some would make it worse and should be avoided.

Palmore, E. (1988). Response to "The Factor Structure of the FAQ" [Letter to the editor]. *The Gerontologist, 28*, 125–126.

Attempts to determine how many factors or subscales there are in the quiz are irrelevant to its reliability, validity, and usefulness as a research tool. Reliability defined as consistency with which similar scores result for similar individuals, or as consistency with which comparable educational groups have similar mean scores, or as consistency with which the most frequent misconceptions are identified; or as test-retest reliability—all show high reliability. The face validity of the quiz is established by the statistics and studies cited in the documentation. Therefore, the quiz is useful for both educational and research purposes.

Palmore, E. (1990). Corrections and comments on Kline's Knowledge of Aging and the Elderly quiz. *Educational Gerontology, 16*, 645–646.

Several errors and dubious assumptions in the KAE quiz were pointed out. The idea that the number of positive valence items should be balanced by an equal number of negative items is theoretically a good idea; however, it does not seem to make much difference in practice. Experiment 1 simply showed that college students can perceive the positive or negative valence of many of the items and can, therefore, bias their answers when told to do so. Because of these errors and lack of substantial differences in mean scores, the KAE does not appear to be an improvement over the FAQ.

Palmore, E. (1992). Knowledge about aging: What we know and need to know. *The Gerontologist, 32*, 149–150.

This editorial reviews what we know about knowledge about aging: The average person with high school education has almost as many misconceptions about correct items of information; the average college student has misconceptions on about one third of the items; the average person tends to have more anti-aged bias than pro-aged bias; knowledge about aging can reduce bias against the aged; the only variables that consistently relate to knowledge are education and attitudes. It also suggests what we need to know: Would a multiple-choice format be worthwhile? Can improvements in knowledge and attitudes change behavior? What are the most cost-effective ways of improving knowledge and attitudes? What are the trends in knowledge and attitudes?

Perrotta, P., Perkins, D., Schimpfhauser, R., & Calkins, E. (1981). Medical student attitudes toward geriatric medicine and patients. *Journal of Medical Education, 56*, 478–483.

This study examines how factual knowledge of the aged, general attitudes toward the aged, and personal contact with the aged influence first-year medical students' attitudes toward geriatric patients and geriatric medicine. The subjects were the entire entering class at the State University of New York at Buffalo School of Medicine in 1979 (N = 127).

Instruments used were the FAQ 1; questions about contact with the aged; the Kogan (1961) attitude scale; and questions about attitudes toward geriatric patients and geriatric medicine.

Eight percent expressed some interest in specializing in geriatric medicine, but only 3% were "very interested" in specializing in geriatrics. Only 4% stated that they would prefer to treat elderly patients instead of younger patients, whereas 48% preferred younger patients. In general, however, students did not express negative attitudes toward elderly patients.

Students had a mean score on the FAQ1 of 63% correct. Regression analyses revealed that the five contact variables failed to account for a significant portion of the variance in knowledge of the aged or in attitudes toward the aged. Knowledge of the aged did not account for a significant portion of the variance of any of the variables assessing attitudes toward geriatric medicine and geriatric patients. It was related significantly, however, to attitudes toward the aged (Kogan's scale, $r = -.43$); that is, the more knowledge the more positive the attitudes.

Patwell, T. (1991). *Attitudes toward and knowledge about the elderly among acute-care nursing staff.* M.S. research paper, University of Wisconsin–Madison School of Nursing, Madison.

The FAQ1 was administered to more than 200 nurses in a midwestern community/teaching hospital before and after a yearlong aging awareness program. There were no significant gains in knowledge or in attitudes. There was a low ($r = .16$) positive correlation between attitude and knowledge score on pre-test, but not at post-test. Knowledge scores were not significantly different by age but were by education. Also participation in certain programs on gerontological practice had higher attitude and knowledge scores.

Pulliam, S., & Dancer, J. (1996). Performance on the Facts on Aging Quiz 2 by undergraduate and graduate students in communicative disorders. *Psychological Reports, 78*, 66.

The FAQ2 was administered to 20 undergraduates, 20 first-semester graduate students, and to 20 graduate students finishing up their degrees. There were no significant differences among the three groups, with all scoring less than 60% correct. It was concluded that the audiology and speech pathology students are not learning the facts on aging as they progress through their training.

Rabins, P., & Motts, Z. (1981). Changing staff attitudes encountered in establishing a psychogeriatric unit. *Hospital & Community Psychiatry, 32*, 729–730.

The FAQ1 was administered to nine nonphysician staff members (nurses and aides) of a 10-bed psychiatric unit that was chosen to become the psychogeriatric unit. The test was given before the changeover and at a 6-month follow-up. The staff was given teaching conferences on psychogeriatrics and cared for geriatric patients during the 6-month interval. The FAQ1 was also administered to a control group, composed of the 62 nonphysician staff members of the other five inpatient psychiatric units in the hospital (Johns Hopkins).

The scores on the first administration were similar for the psychogeriatric staff and the control staff (62% and 61% correct, respectively). On the follow-up administration, the mean score for the psychogeriatric unit increased to 73% correct, whereas that of the control group increased only slightly, to 62%. The difference between the groups' scores at follow-up was statistically significant.

The scores of the staff on the first administration were similar to those obtained by Holtzman and Beck (1981) from similarly trained individuals, which indicates that these staff members did not have special interest in or knowledge about the elderly before the unit's establishment. Rabins and Motts conclude in this study that contact with the elderly through patient care and teaching conferences results in increased knowledge about aging.

Ramon, P. (1986). *Knowledge about aging among nursing home staff.* Unpublished manuscript.

This study was held in three nursing homes in Durham, NC, where 32 registered nurses (RNs) and licensed practical nurses (LPNs) answered the FAQ1. The mean number of correct answers for the RNs was 18; it was 14 for the LPNs. The most common mistakes among both groups were on Items 7, 16, 19, 21, and 23 to 25. The LPNs also had 73% incorrect on Item 11, whereas only 23% of the RNs got that item wrong. This was attributed to the greater contact with older nursing home patients by the LPNs compared with the RNs. Because nursing home patients tend to be unable to adapt to change, the LPNs tended to generalize from their patients to all aged and answer that the aged are unable to adapt to change.

Ramoth, J. (1985, June 3). *Knowledge of aging among teacher education students.* Unpublished letter to E. Palmore.

Teacher-education undergraduate students at Kean College of New Jersey ($N = 345$) were tested with the FAQ1 and Kogan's (1961) scale. The mean score was 55% correct, with the number of correct responses ranging from 4 to 21. The majority missed 14 of the items. The aged net bias score was –3 on the FAQ1; however, on Kogan's scale there was a slightly favorable mean attitude score toward the aged.

Richardson, C. (1993). Utilizing curriculum to effect a change in the attitudes, knowledge, and interactions of community college students with the elderly. *Dissertation Abstracts International, 54–10A*, 3845.

The FAQ was used to assess the effects of an educational intervention on aging with an experimental group of 30 students and 31 students in a control group in English classes. The mean percentage score on the FAQ was only 46% (below the chance score of 50%). There was an increase in knowledge by all students. There was negative correlation between semesters completed and knowledge which suggests that students have been exposed to inaccurate information in their curriculum. Changes in attitudes toward the elderly as the result of increased knowledge, and experience with the aged were more positive than negative. It was concluded that curriculum seeking to increase knowledge about aging and provide experience with the aged will be most effective in developing positive attitudes toward elderly persons.

Riddick, C. (1985). The impact of an in-service educational program on the gerontological knowledge and attitudes of geriatric recreational service providers. *Educational Gerontology, 11*, 127–135.

A nonequivalent–control-group design was used. The experimental group was made up of 20 attendees of the Leisure and Aging Management School at the University of Maryland. The control group was an outdoor resource management class of 16 undergraduates. The in-service educational program was designed for geriatric recreational service providers.

The experimental group underwent a significant increase in gerontological knowledge (from 74% to 94% correct on the FAQ1). The control group showed no change (57% at both testings). Neither group experienced a significant change in their attitudes.

The amount of change in knowledge was significantly influenced by the degree of contact with elders, but not by educational background. At the same time, change in attitudes toward elders was not associated with degree of contact or educational background.

Robertson, J. (1991). *Knowledge of aging: A study of university students enrolled in introductory level psychology courses.* Abstract of Ph.D. dissertation in health education, Southern Illinois University, Carbondale.

The FAQ1 was administered to 542 students in introductory level psychology courses. Knowledge was higher among older students and whites. Scoring the quiz with the DK option increased the internal reliability.

Romeis, J., & Sussman, M. (1980). Cross-cultural differences on the Facts on Aging Quiz. *Aging and Society, 2*, 357–370.

This report using the FAQ1 compares responses from U.S. (N = 206) and Japanese (N = 591) samples, thus adding a cross-cultural dimension to the literature on age bias measurement. The U.S. group was a random sample of married persons aged 20 and over from Forsyth County, NC. The Japanese were a random sample of married persons aged 20 to 49, living in Tokyo.

The data indicate that the FAQ1 is a reliable measure, but the validity of the measure's age bias dimension is more complex than previously indicated. Because four of the five pro-aged statements reflect physical capacity, and the majority of the anti-aged bias statements reflect psychological and social capacity, a simple subtraction of the percentage of anti-aged items missed from the percentage of pro-aged items missed may not be a valid measure of age bias.

The percentage distribution of correct answers by the U.S. sample closely resembles that of Klemmack (1978). The average percentage correct was identical in these two samples (57%). Sixteen statements differed by only 4%. Three statements, however, differed by 16% or more: Items 2, 23, and 25. However, the total response distributions indicate an acceptable descriptive reliability.

In comparing the Japanese and U.S. groups, many more of the responses vary significantly. Fifteen of the items were statistically different, even though the average total percentages correct were similar (53% and 55%, respectively). The Japanese sample was found to be significantly more anti-aged biased: The aged net bias scores were –39 for the Japanese and –18 for the U.S. citizens. This is contrary to the expectation that the Japanese would have more positive attitudes toward aging and the aged. This may be explained by subtle changes that occur in the translation, which may somehow increase the percentage of "errors" in

Japan. Also the falsity or truth of some of the items may vary between the two populations. Some of the items cannot be verified in Japan because of lack of research there.

Ross, M. (1983). Learning to nurse the elderly: Outcome measures. *Journal of Advanced Nursing, 8*, 373–378.

This study explores the impact of a planned learning experience with the elderly on nursing students' level of knowledge about aging. The FAQ 1 was administered to 64 students before and after an experience of contact with well older people who were living independently. The mean percentage correct increased significantly after the experience (from 66% to 80%). The aged net bias score was slightly negative but did not change significantly (–5 to –9). The majority of students had incorrect answers on the pretest on Items 7, 16, 17, 19, 21, 23, and 24.

Rydman, L. (1986). Knowledge of the aging process and the aged among clerical and technical health care workers. Unpublished master's thesis, Health Sciences Center, University of Illinois, Chicago.

The knowledge about aging of clerical and technical health care workers at an urban outpatient center was studied. Subjects completed the FAQ1 and a questionnaire about demographic information and personal and work experience with the elderly. Clerical and technical employees correctly answered 60% of the items. The more educated respondents scored higher. The instrument was useful as a stimulant for group discussion and clarification of the common misconceptions that this employee group held about the aged.

Sakata, S., & Okamoto, T. (1985). The attitude of caregivers toward their work with the aged in nursing homes and factors influencing that attitude. *Social Gerontology, 22*, 99–100.

This article is aimed at clarifying the structure of the attitude of caregivers toward working with the aged in nursing homes and at determining the important factors that influence that attitude. The sample included 563 caregivers in 21 nursing homes in Tokyo. Attitude was measured by the Work With the Aged Scale developed by Kahana and Kiyak (1984). Knowledge was measured by the FAQ1. Lower self-estimation of social status as a caregiver (factor 1) was found among those with a higher education and who had more knowledge of aging. Conversely, higher estimation of social status was found in those who expressed a more negative attitude toward aging as measured by Palmore's negative-bias score.

Tension or frustration in working with the aged (factor 2) were more strongly felt by those who had a more negative attitude toward aging and had greater dissatisfaction with their supervisors and coworkers. A more positive attitude toward social welfare services for the aged (factor 3) was expressed by those who (a) were younger, (b) had a higher education, (c) were more desirous of having the present job, (d) had been in the present job for a shorter period, (e) had more knowledge of aging, and (f) had greater satisfaction with work hours.

Satterfield, M., Yasumara, K., & Goodman, G. (1984). Impact of an engineered physical therapy program for the elderly. *International Journal of Rehabilitation Research, 7*, 151–152.

An 8-week pilot study was conducted at McDonald Army Hospital, Physical Therapy Clinic, Fort Eustis, VA, to evaluate the effectiveness of an engineered pool therapy program for resolving the inadequacies of failing to provide the elderly with care that incorporated a total concept of health, in a situation in which staffing was a constraint. It was designed to change misconceptions about aging, create a viable social network through group instructional strategy, and improve physical fitness. A small, nonrandom sample of 10 participants was selected for the pilot program. The FAQ1 was administered as a pretest and posttest, to assess attitudinal changes. Physical measurements of strength, range of motion, flexibility, or endurance, as applicable, were documented. Calculated pairing of participants based on similar disability but dissimilar age category constituted the key difference between this pool program and a traditional pool program.

There was a significant impact of this program on endurance performance but no impact on attitudinal changes. However, attributing this significant improvement of physical fitness exclusively to the engineered pool program design would be premature. Further investigations using randomized sampling and a control group were recommended.

Sheeley, E. (1979, January 22). *Knowledge of aging among nursing students*. Unpublished letter to E. Palmore.

Nursing students ($N = 24$) in a course on gerontology had a mean score on the FAQ1 of 72% correct. Most errors were on Items 16, 19, 21, 23, and 24.

Shenk, D., Lee, J. (1995). Meeting the educational needs of service providers: Effects of a continuing education program on self-reported knowledge and attitudes about aging. *Educational Gerontology, 21*, 671–681.

The FAQ was used to evaluate the effectiveness of a continuing education program called the Professional Development Program in Gerontology. Results show that the program was successful at improving the Ss' attitudes toward aging and knowledge of professional service providers to older adults.

Singleton, J., Harbison, J., Melanson, P., & Jackson, G. (1993). A study of the factual knowledge and common misperceptions about aging held by health care professionals. *Activities, Adaptation & Aging, 18*, 37–47.

The study determined knowledge levels of 66 dentists, 68 nurses, 52 activity directors (ATDs), 67 dental hygienists (DHs) and 41 social workers (SWs) regarding elderly individuals (EIs). Ss completed a questionnaire that included the FAQ. All professional groups demonstrated some age biases. Only 95 Ss were aware of the rate of institutionalization among EIs. The majority of nurses, dentists, and DHs did not agree that medical practitioners gave low priority to EIs. However, 77% of ATDs and 66% of SWs believed that EIs were given low priority. The majority of Ss believe that EIs were more underprivileged than they actually were, and the majority of Ss in all groups except SWs believed that EIs became more religious as they aged.

Smith, M. (1985). *The changing attitudes of the physical therapy student toward the geriatric patient.* Unpublished manuscript.

This study was designed to measure the attitude of undergraduate physical therapy students toward the geriatric population, over the course of a 2-year physical therapy curriculum. The FAQ1 was administered to three consecutive classes entering the University of Pittsburgh Program in Physical Therapy, at various points during their program.

The most common misconceptions (those with a majority giving incorrect answers) were Items 7, 16, 19, 21, and 24. The mean score for the various groups tended to increase from 65% correct at the beginning of the program to 77% at the end. The net bias score was consistently negative, ranging from –1 to –24, but did not show any consistent pattern of change; that is, two classes tended to decrease and one increased.

Smith, M., Fincham, J., Ladner, K., & O'Quin, J. (1989). Mississippi pharmacists' scores on the FAQ. *Journal of Geriatric Drug Therapy, 14*, 91–98.

The FAQ2 was administered to 400 Mississippi pharmacists as part of a pretest in a geriatric education program. The majority of the pharmacists correctly answer only half of the 25 questions. One third of the questions were answered incorrectly a second time by those completing the education program ($N = 34$). There was a 24% negative bias toward the aged.

Steel, L. (1987). Dental students' attitudes and knowledge about elderly people. *Gerondontics, 3*, 61–64.

A study of final-year dental students in 3 British and 1 Irish dental school looked at attitudes and knowledge about the elderly, misconceptions, and level of experience with elderly people. Physics students were used for comparison. The FAQ1 was modified to be suitable for use in the United Kingdom. All groups of students had positive attitudes to younger people, some negative or neutral attitudes to older people, but the physics students had positive attitudes to older people. The physics students were slightly more knowledgeable (63% correct) than the dental students (59% correct).

Steinhauer, M., & Brockway, J. (1980). The impact of gerontological education: Knowledge and attitudes of public management students toward the elderly. In I. Wittels & J. Hendricks (Eds.), *Gerontology tomorrow: Consolidation/expansion?* Washington, DC: Association for Gerontology in Higher Education.

The effect of gerontology courses on public management students' knowledge about and attitudes toward the elderly was explored. The FAQ1 and Rosencranz and McNevin's (1969) Aging-Semantic Differential Scale were administered to students both before and after a gerontology course. There were 66 experimental subjects and 21 control subjects (not exposed to the course). Students' ages ranged from 21 to 74 years.

For both pretest and posttest, correct knowledge about aging was associated with a positive attitude toward the elderly. The student's age was directly related to positive attitudes, and females had a slightly more positive attitude than did males. Students who were exposed to the gerontological course showed positive attitudinal and knowledge changes between pretest and posttest, and control students' attitudes remained about the same. It was concluded that gerontological course work should be incorporated into the curriculum of public management education.

Stone, V. (1977). *Knowledge of aging among undergraduate and faculty nurses*. Unpublished table.

The FAQ1 was given to 30 undergraduate nursing students and 10 faculty members at the Duke University School of Nursing. The nursing students had a mean score of 66% correct, and the faculty had 78% correct. The most frequent errors (with over 50% wrong) among the students were on Items 7, 16, 17, 18, 19, 21, 23, and 24. The faculty had over 50% errors on the same items except for Items 17, 18, and 23.

Strayer, M., DiAngelis, A., & Loupe, M. (1987). Ohio dentists' knowledge and perceptions of the elderly. *Ohio Dental Journal, 61*, 20–24.

The FAQ1 was administered to 464 general practice dentists in Ohio. The mean correct score was 66%, which was similar to those reported for medical students, dental students, and physicians. Over 95% overestimated the size of the elderly population, more than 80% felt the majority were bored, and over 60% overestimated the number of elderly in long-term care institutions. There were no significant differences between dentists of different ages that indicate that despite increased interest in aging, there is no substantial difference in knowledge between older & younger dentists.

Stum, M. (1993). Knowledge of aging of subsidized housing managers for the elderly: Implications for training. *Educational Gerontology, 19*, 127–138.

Investigated knowledge of aging as one indicator of how prepared managers of housing (HMs) are to handle aging-in-place elderly. 160 HMs for the elderly were surveyed on their knowledge and assumptions about aging using the FAQ1. Differences in HMs' knowledge as influenced by their characteristics and environments were also examined. HMs' knowledge appears to be similar to that of other service provider groups. HMs held several misconceptions concerning the elderly that included a lack of understanding about their health and socioeconomic status. Training in aging and experience were positively related to increased knowledge about aging. The best predictors of knowledge were the level of services to the elderly in the community and the time spent in the position of manager.

Sussman, M., Romeis, J., & Maeda, D. (1980). Age bias in Japan: Implications for normative conflict. *International Review of Modern Sociology, 10*, 243–254.

This article is based on the same data as reported in Romeis and Sussman (1980). It presents an alternative method of computing the net bias score: The number of negative-bias errors is subtracted from the number of positive-bias errors, and 16 is added to the result, thus eliminating any negative numbers. Thus, net-bias scores could range from 0 (anti-aging) to 21 (pro-aging). The advantage of this method is that it gives each item equal weight, whereas the Palmore method gives three times as much weight to each pro-aging item because there are only one third (5) as many pro-aging items as there are anti-aging items (16). Using this alternative method the Winston-Salem sample had a net bias score of 10, which was only 2 points more than the Japanese score of 8. By comparison, the Palmore method makes the Japanese appear to be twice as anti-aged (–39) as the Winston-Salem sample (–18).

The Japanese sample tended to describe correctly the declining physical capacities of the aged but was factually incorrect in stating marked declines in psychological and social capacity. The implications for normative conflict in Japan are discussed.

Swaykus, M. (1987). *Knowledge about aging and mental health among nurses and aides in nursing homes*. Unpublished table.

The FAMHQ was administered to 9 registered nurses, 31 licensed practical nurses, and 97 nurses aides in six nursing homes in Kingsport, TN.

DK responses were allowed. The registered nurses had the highest average score (68% correct), followed by the licensed practical nurses (65%), and the nurses aides (60%). This probably reflects the relative amount of professional training in these three groups. The items with less than 50% correct were 2, 4, 6, 7, 12 (only 10% correct), 19, 20, 22, and 23.

Thompson, P. (1983). *Facts on aging quiz: Issues of linguistic and cultural translation*. Paper presented at 1983 annual meeting of the Gerontological Society of America in San Francisco.

The FAQ1 was translated into Portuguese and administered to 61 university students. One week later the English version was administered to the same students and the answers compared to the answers given to the Portuguese version. Differences between responses of Portuguese, American, and Japanese students are also discussed.

Tojo, M., & Maeda, D. (1985). Attitude of caregivers in nursing homes as measured by the Job Description Index. *Social Gerontology, 22*, 98–99.

The major purpose of this series of studies on caregivers in nursing homes was to reveal the attitude of caregivers toward various elements of their work and to determine the important factors that influence these attitudes. The sample was composed of 563 caregivers working in 21 Tokyo nursing homes. Interviews included the FAQ1 and the Job Description Index (JDI) used in Kahana and Kiyak's (1984) study, and modified to make it suitable for Japan. Considering the total JDI score, the job satisfaction of the caregivers was fairly high. The section on "Work Itself" satisfaction was significantly higher when the respondent got a lower score on the FAQ1 and when the aged net-bias score was less negative. The section on "pay" satisfaction was significantly higher when the respondent's attitude toward aging was more negative.

Tyson, S. (1992). *The design, implementation and evaluation of a faculty development program in gerontological nursing*. Ed.D. dissertation, New York City Technical College, City University of New York, New York.

Measurement of the effects of receiving knowledge and information about aging was carried out with a group of 12 nurse faculty who participated in a series of eight workshops on gerontological nursing. A comparison group consisted of six nurse faculty who taught in another school of nursing and were matched for geographic location, student demographics and faculty credentials. The FAQ2 and FAMHQ were administered before and after the period of instruction on gerontological nursing. Results showed that knowledge on aging in both treatment and control groups improved slightly, although the improvement was not significantly different between the two groups.

Wallace, R. W., & Wallace, R. K. (1982). Assessing clergy's knowledge of aging: Suggestions for training. *Gerontology and Geriatrics Education, 2*, 285–290.

The FAQ 1 was sent to a sample of Protestant ministers in a large midwestern city; 201 completed tests were returned (68%). The mean score was 66% correct, which was somewhat lower than that for other professionals with graduate-level training reported by Palmore (1977). The majority missed Items 1, 5, 8, 15, 16, 20, and 24. Respondents who were non-white, less educated, and members of the National Baptist denomination tended to have less knowledge of aging. Also, respondents who had prior training in aging were more knowledgeable and tended to have special programs for their older members. These findings suggest that, with training in gerontology, ministers become more knowledgeable or sensitized to the needs of the elderly, with this awareness being shown by the special programs for the elderly.

Walter, M. (1986). Biases and misconceptions of nurses toward the elderly. Unpublished manuscript.

Misconceptions and biases toward the elderly of 167 nurses employed in long-term-care institutions were examined using the FAQ1. Independent variables were years employed as a nurse, age, amount of continuing education in gerontology, gerontology courses in nursing school, basic nursing education, percentage of caseload over age 65, and type of facility. The study replicated McDowell's (1978) study of community nurses.

There were seven major findings: (a) Nurses employed in private institutions had significantly more biases and misconceptions than nurses employed in nonprofit or public institutions. (b) The total mean score was 63% correct. (c) Continuing education had no effect on biases and misconceptions of the nurses. (d) The nurses had more negative biases (38%) than positive biases (26%). (e) Nurses under age 35 had fewer misconceptions and biases than older nurses. (f) Nurses employed less than 10 years had fewer positive biases than nurses employed longer. (g) Nurses working in long-term-care institutions held more biases and misconceptions than nurses employed in home health or ambulatory care centers.

West, H., & Ernst, M. (1981). The life enrichment program for older adults: An alternative educational model. *Educational Gerontology, 7*, 257–274.

This article is a review of an experimental educational program designed to provide experiential activities related to learning needs and potentials of older adults. Eighteen persons over age 57 participated in the experiment. Pretest and posttest measures were made with the FAQ1 and several attitude scales. There were also pretest and posttest measures of such physiological functions as weight, blood pressure, and pulse rate.

As a result of the program, morale and locus of control increased significantly. Knowledge of aging and purpose in life also increased but not enough to be statistically significant. Body fat and weight declined significantly. Pulse rate also declined but not significantly. Systolic blood pressure declined significantly. All participants stated that their level of well-being had improved.

West, H., & Levy, W. (1981). Knowledge of aging in an elderly population. *Research on Aging, 3*, 202–210.

The FAQ1 was given to 164 older people attending programs on aging information. The older persons were not as knowledgeable (56% correct) as the Duke undergraduates in Palmore's (1977) study (65% correct). There were no significant differences between males and females or old-old and young-old within the older group.

The elderly held similar misconceptions to those of the undergraduates but were slightly less anti-aged in their bias than the undergraduates. Within the elderly group, males and the old-old were more anti-aged than the females and the young-old.

West, H., & Levy, W. (1984). Knowledge of aging in the medical profession. *Gerontology and Geriatrics Education, 4*, 23–31.

The FAQ1 was given to 170 physicians to determine level of knowledge, common misconceptions, and aging bias.

The physicians' knowledge of aging was similar to that of undergraduate students reported by Palmore (1977): 68% and 66% correct, respectively. The most frequent misconceptions were also similar in the two groups: Item 19 was most often missed by both groups, and a majority also missed Items 2, 7, 16, 21, 23, and 24.

Within the physician group, specialty subgroups had no significant effect on mean scores. The 30- to 39-age cohort scored significantly lower (65%) than other cohorts. The aged net-bias score was negative for all cohorts except the age 60 years and over cohort, among whom it was +2; and it was negative for all specialties except internal medicine, for which it was neutral. Thus, it appears that specialists in internal medicine who are age 60 years or older know more about aging and are less negative toward the aged than others. Implications for medical education in gerontology are noted.

Wexler, E. (1979, January 22). *Knowledge about aging among public health nurses*. Unpublished letter to E. Palmore.

The FAQ1 was given to a random sample of 100 public health nurses from six health units in Greater Toronto, Canada. The wording of some items was changed to make them applicable to Canada. Most of the nurses carried older persons in their caseload. Most also had experienced some type of gerontological education in the past 5 years, the most frequent type being personal reading (71%), followed by team conferences (44%).

The mean score was 68% correct. There were no significant differences by agency. Items on which more than 50% were wrong were 7, 16, 17, 19, 21, 24, and 25.

Whittington, F. (1978). *Knowledge of aging among nursing students*. Unpublished table.

The FAQ1 was given to 19 senior nursing students at Georgia State University. The mean score was 68% correct. Items with over 50% wrong were 2, 7, 16,17, 1 9, 21, 23, and 24. All of the students incorrectly thought over 15% of the U.S. population is over age 65 (Item 19).

Williams, A. (1982). *A comparison of attitudes toward aging between types of nurses*. Unpublished manuscript.

This is a report of a comparison of attitudes toward aging between two levels of nurses—registered nurses and licensed practical nurses—who worked in two kinds of health care settings, long-term care ($N = 47$) and acute care hospitals ($N = 59$). Attitudes were measured by the FAQ 1. Findings confirmed previous studies that the majority (75%) had negative attitudes toward aging and older adults. In addition, the scores for this population were within the range found among other nurse populations.

Older nurses were found to be significantly less negative toward aging and older people. Nurses working in long-term-care geriatric settings were more negative than were nurses in acute care settings. LPNs were significantly less negative toward aging than were the RNs; however, RNs were significantly more knowledgeable about aging than were LPNs. White nurses were significantly more knowledgeable about aging than were Black nurses. There was a significant increase in knowledge about aging in the group who attended two or more workshops or courses in gerontology.

Wicker, C. (1995). *Ageism and the American dream: The administration of the FAQ in a multicultural setting*. Unpublished research project for the master's of social work program at the University of Hawaii School of Social Work.

The FAQ1 was administered to undergraduates at the University of Hawaii to evaluate whether those with Asian and Pacific Island background hold their elders in higher esteem than do Whites. Results were unavailable in 1997.

Williams, R., Lusk, S., & Kline, N. (1986). Knowledge of aging and cognitive styles in baccalaureate nursing students. *The Gerontologist, 26*, 545–550.

Factual knowledge and attitudes toward the elderly were examined for relationships with academic achievement, experience, and cognitive styles among 322 nursing students at the University of Michigan.

The instruments used were the FAQ1, a questionnaire on experience with the aged, and several attitude scales. The mean score on the FAQ1 was 70% correct, which was significantly higher than the score for undergraduate students reported by Palmore (1977). A significant correlation ($r = .36$) was found between the grade point average of the students and their knowledge of aging. The aged net bias score was –9, which was similar to that reported by Palmore.

Experience with elderly people did not predict knowledge about aging. Cognitive style and knowledge were not significantly correlated. However, students expressing a preference for the older client seemed to be more knowledgeable and less negatively biased toward this population.

Wilson, R., & Glamser, R. (1982). The impact of a gerontological intervention on osteopathic medical students. *Educational Gerontology, 8*, 373–380.

To evaluate the impact of adding a brief unit on aging to the first-year curriculum of a school of osteopathic medicine, a quasi-experimental design was employed. The educational experience involved 3 hours of classroom material, a visit to a nursing home, and a visit to a congregate housing facility for the well elderly. During one semester, the entire first-year class ($N = 82$) was scheduled for the program. The instruments were the FAQ 1 and the Aging Semantic Differential Scale (Rosencranz & McNevin, 1969). There was no control group.

There was a mild but significant improvement in knowledge and attitudes between the pretest and posttest. The mean score increased from 62% to 66% correct. Two of the three subscales of the Aging Semantic Differential Scale also showed improvements that were statistically significant. There was also an improvement of 10 points on the total attitude scale. Student reaction to the program was very positive.

Wirth, J. (1987, November). Ageism: Predictors and trends (1980–1985). Paper prepared for the Gerontological Society of America Annual Meeting.

The FAQ1 was administered to a 1980 sample of 758 college students and a 1985 sample of 545 college students. Ageism was defined as the number of misconceptions that respondents had on the FAQ1. There was more ageism among college students who had parents with lower levels of education, and among students who were less academically oriented or informed: vocational-type students, younger students, students with lower grade point averages, students perceiving general educational requirements to be a waste of time, and students having aspirations for a low-prestige job on graduation. There were also relationships between prejudicial attitudes on minorities and ageism. A multiple regression of significant variables related to ageism found that ageism was most predicted by materialistic values, lower socioeconomic status, and a deemphasis on personal relationships.

Wolk, M. (1986). *Gerontological knowledge of nursing students.* Unpublished manuscript.

The purpose of this study was to determine differences in the gerontological knowledge of senior students in associate and baccalaureate degree nursing programs and students studying for a master of science degree in nursing in southwest Florida. Thirty associate-degree students, 30 baccalaureate-degree students, and 30 master's-degree students filled out the FAQ2. Demographic data were also collected. There were no significant differences in knowledge among the three groups. The study concluded that the advanced educational level of these nurses did not increase gerontological knowledge.

Youngman, B. (1980). *Clergy and nonclergy's beliefs and knowledge about old people.* Unpublished doctoral dissertation, Michigan State University, East Lansing.

One of the objectives of this study was to define knowledge about the elderly among clergy and nonclergy and to determine the effect on each group of one type of planned learning experience. There were 64 subjects, and 26 clergy and 38 nonclergy church leaders, who were participants in two "Workshops for Religious Leadership on Aging." The FAQ1 was administered as a pretest and posttest to measure change in knowledge.

The clergy group had a significant increase in mean score, from 66% correct to 71%. The small increase for nonclergy (67% to 68%) was not significant.

Zigarmi, D. (1986). *Middle school students' attitudes toward the aged.* Unpublished manuscript.

The focus of the study was to measure change in student attitudes and knowledge that occurred as a result of a 5-week interdisciplinary unit on aging. The two tests given were a semantic differential, to measure affect, and a modified FAQ1, to measure cognitive changes. There were 174 students from 6th to 8th grades, and they were divided into treatment and control groups.

A Multiple Hierarchical Analysis was performed to develop four subscales: Comparison (differences between younger and older people), State of Being (stereotypes about older persons' existential condition), Work Skills and Desires (stereotypes about older persons' attitudes and capacities toward work), and Health and Social Conditions (stereotypes about older persons' health or social conditions in the present or future). The internal consistency reliability coefficients (Kuder-Richardson 20 analysis) were .79, .70, .59, and .53, respectively.

Knowledge about aging did improve after the unit on aging: The mean score increased from 61% to 69% correct (significant at $p = .001$). All of the subscales also increased, but the Comparison subscale increase was not significant. Attitudes toward older people also improved significantly.

References

Adelman, R., & Albert, R. (1987). Medical students attitudes toward the elderly. *Gerontology and Geriatrics Education, 7,* 141–155.

Allen, B. (1981). Knowledge of aging: A cross-sectional study of three different age groups. *Educational Gerontology, 6,* 49.

Anderson, R., Kochanek, K., & Murphy, S. (1997). Report of final mortality statistics, 1995. *Monthly Vital Statistics Report, 45* (Suppl. 2).

Anonymous. (1986). *Negatively biased misconceptions about old age and aging in Japanese adults.* Unpublished manuscript, Tokyo Metropolitan Institute of Gerontology, Tokyo, Japan.

Anonymous. (1992). Effects of a geriatric course on knowledge about aging among optometry students. Unpublished manuscript submitted to *The Gerontologist.*

Ansello, E., & Lamy, P. (1987). Geropharmacy and gerontology for rural community pharmacists. Unpublished report to the AARP Andrus Foundation from the Center on Aging, University of Maryland, College Park, MD.

Atchley, R. (1996). *Social forces and aging*. Belmont, CA: Wadsworth.

Ausherman, J. (1991). Junior high school health teachers' knowledge and attitudes about aging and implementation of aging education. *Educational Gerontology, 17,* 391–401.

Barefoot, J. (1995). Hostility. In G. Maddox (Ed.), *The encyclopedia of aging.* NY: Springer.

Barnet, M. (1979). *Contact with elderly persons as a correlate of knowledge about aging*. Unpublished master's thesis, Boston University, Boston.

Barresi, C., & Brubaker, T. (1979). Clinical social workers' knowledge about aging: Responses to the "Facts on Aging Quiz." *Journal of Gerontological Social Work, 2,* 137–146.

Baugher, E., & Lamison-White, L. (1996). *Poverty in the U.S: Current population reports* (Series 60-194). Washington: Government Printing Office.

Belgrave, L., Lavin, B., Breslau, N., & Haug, M. (1982). Stereotyping of the aged by medical students. *Gerontology and Geriatrics Education, 3*, 37–44.

Blackwell, D. (1979, January 22). *Effects of a workshop on aging on knowledge about aging*. Unpublished letter to E. Palmore.

Blazer, D., & Palmore, E. (1976). Religion and aging in a longitudinal panel. *The Gerontologist, 16*, 82–85.

Blazer, D., & George, L. (1995). NIMH Epidemiologic Catchment Area Project. In G. Maddox (Ed.), *The encyclopedia of aging*. NY: Springer.

Bond, S. (1979, January 28). *Knowledge about aging among participants in retirement planning courses*. Unpublished letter to E. Palmore.

Bressler, D. (1996). Occupational therapists' knowledge on aging. Master's Thesis, Levin School of Health Sciences, Touro College.

Broder, H., & Block, M. (1986, July-August). Effects of geriatric education on the knowledge of dental students. *Special Care in Dentistry*, 177–179.

Brown, I. (1993). Ageism in American culture: Patterns of prejudice and discrimination by the dominant group and its effects on older African-Americans. PhD Dissertation, Union Institute Graduate School, Cincinnati, OH.

Brubaker, T., & Barresi, C. (1979). Social workers' level of knowledge about old age and perceptions of service delivery to the elderly. *Research on Aging, 1*, 213–232.

Burris, R. (1992). Measuring the learning outcomes of a continuing education seminar about the aging process on the knowledge level of registered nurses. *Dissertation Abstracts International, 53-12A*, 4169.

Butler, R. (1995). Mental health and illness. In G. Maddox (Ed.), *The encyclopedia of aging*. NY: Springer.

Byrd, M. (1984). Personal growth aspects of peer counselor training for older adults. *Educational Gerontology, 10*, 369–385.

Carver, R. (1974). Two dimensions of tests: Psychometric and edumetric. *American Psychologist, 29*, 512–518.

Carmel, S., Cwikel, J., & Galinody, D. (1992). Changes in knowledge, attitudes, and work preferences following courses in gerontology among medical, nursing, and social work students. *Educational Gerontology, 18*, 329–342

Carmel, S., Galinsky, D., & Cwikel, J. (1990). Knowledge, attitudes, and work preferences regarding the elderly among medical students and practicing physicians. *Behavior, Health, & Aging, 1*, 99–104.

Cerella, J. (1995). In G. Maddox (Ed.), *The encyclopedia of aging*. NY: Springer.

Chandler, J., Rachal, J., & Kazelskis, R. (1986). Attitudes of long-term care nursing personnel toward the elderly. Unpublished letter to Palmore.

Clark, M. (1996). Measuring facts and views of aging with Palmore's quizzes. Abstract in *The Gerontologist, 36,* Special Issue 1: 375.

Clark, R. (1995). Economics. In G. Maddox (Ed.), *The encyclopedia of aging.* NY: Springer.

Coe, R., Miler, D., Prendergast, J., & Grossberg, G. (1982). Faculty resources for teaching geriatric medicine. *Journal of the American Geriatrics Society, 30*, 63–66.

Cole, D., & Dancer, J. (1996). Comparison of four health-care disciplines on the Facts on Aging and Mental Health Quiz. *Psychological Reports, 79,* 350.

Courtenay, B., & Suhart, M. (1980). *Myths and realities of aging.* Athens: Georgia Center for Continuing Education.

Courtenay, B., & Weidemann, C. (1985). The effects of a "don't know" response on Palmore's Facts on Aging Quizzes. *The Gerontologist, 25*, 177–181.

Coward, R., & Netzer, J. (1995). Coresidence. In G. Maddox (Ed.), *The encyclopedia of aging*. NY: Springer.

Crown, W. (1995). Income distribution: Effects of government policies. In G. Maddox (Ed.), *The encyclopedia of aging*. NY: Springer.

Cutler, S. (1995). Crime. In G. Maddox (Ed.), *The encyclopedia of aging*. NY: Springer.

Dail, P., & Johnson, J. (1985). Measuring change in undergraduate students' perception about aging. *Gerontology and Geriatric Education, 5*, 4.

Doka, K. (1986). Adolescent attitudes and beliefs toward aging and the elderly. *International Journal of Aging and Human Development, 22*, 173–187.

Donnelly, M., Duthie, E., Kirsling, R., & Gambert, S. (1985). *Measuring knowledge gain in geriatric medical education: Analysis of an instrument.* Unpublished manuscript.

Dowd, S. (1983). Radiographers' knowledge of aging. *Radiological Technology, 54*, 192–196.

Dudley, K. (1992). A study of the relationship between death anxiety and negative bias toward the elderly among counselors. M.S. Thesis, Division of Counseling Psychology, University of Oregon.

Duerson, M., Thomas, J., Chang, J., & Stevens, C. (1992). Medical students' knowledge and misconception about aging: Responses to Palmore's FAQ's. *The Gerontologist, 32,* 171–174.

Durand, R., Roff, L., & Klemmack, D. (1981). Cognitive differentiation and the perceptions of older persons. *Research on Aging, 3*, 333–344.

Duthie, E., & Gambert, S. (1983). The impact of a geriatric medicine rotation on internal medicine resident knowledge of aging. *Gerontology and Geriatric Education, 3*, 233–236.

Dye, C., & Sassenrath, D. (1979). Identification of normal aging and disease related processes. *Journal of the American Geriatrics Society, 27*, 472–475.

Eaglestein, A., & Weinsberg, E. (1985). Knowledge and attitudes of teenagers concerning the elderly. Discussion Papers produced by the Joint Israel Brookdale Institute of Gerontology and Adult Human Development in Israel, Jerusalem.

Eakes, G. (1986). *The relationship between death anxiety and attitudes toward the elderly among nursing staff*. Unpublished manuscript.

Earley, L., & von Mering, O. (1969). Growing old the outpatient way. *American Journal of Psychiatry, 125*, 963–967.

Eckel, F. (1977). *Knowledge about aging among pharmacy students*. Unpublished table.

Edwards, M., & Aldous, I. (1996). Attitudes to and knowledge about elderly people: A comparative analysis of students of medicine, English and computer science and their teachers. *Medical Education, 30,* 221–225.

Edwards, R., Plant, M. Novak, D., Beall, C., & Baumhover, L. (1992). Knowledge about aging and Alzheimer's disease among baccalaureate nursing students. *Journal of Nursing Education, 31,* 127–125.

Ellison, J. (1991). A study of corporate managers' knowledge regarding age and of the older worker. *Dissertation Abstracts International, 52-11A,* 4101.

Ellor, J., & Altfeld, S. (1980, November). *Knowledge and attitudes of hospital personnel toward elderly patients*. Paper presented at the annual meeting of the Gerontological Society of America, San Diego.

Eyster, C. (1979, January 28). *Knowledge about aging among high school students*. Unpublished letter to E. Palmore.

Filipcic, S. (1990). Nursing home nurses' knowledge regarding the facts on aging. Master's thesis, Department of Physiological Nursing, University of Washington.

Francis, C. (1991). Assessing knowledge and attitudes about the elderly in acute care hospital and nursing home registered staff nurses. Unpublished abstract of a study in VA Medical Center, East Orange, NJ.

Geboy, M. (1982). Use of the Facts on Aging Quiz in dental education. *Gerontology and Geriatrics Education, 3*, 65–67.

George, L. (1995). Social and economic factors. In E. Busse & D. Blazer (Eds.), *Geriatric psychiatry*. Washington, DC: American Psychiatric Press.

Gibson, J., Choi, Y., & Cook, D. (1993). Service providers knowledge and misconceptions about old age. *Educational Gerontology, 19*, 727–741.

Golde, P., & Kogan, N. (1959). A sentence completion procedure for assessing attitudes toward old people. *Journal of Gerontology, 14*, 355–363.

Goulet, Y. (1982). *Faits concernant l'avance en age: Un bref quiz*. Unpublished translation of FAQ1.

Greenhill, E., & Baker, M. (1986). The effects of a well older adult clinical experience on students' knowledge and attitudes. *Journal of Nursing Education, 25*, 145–147.

Greenslade, V. (1986). *Evaluation of postgraduate gerontological nursing education*. Unpublished manuscript.

Groseck, J. (1989). A study of attitudes Philadelphians have toward old people, their knowledge about aging, and demographic characteristics. *Dissertation Abstracts International, 50-06A,* 1768.

Gurland, B. (1995). Psychopathology. In G. Maddox (Ed.), *The encyclopedia of aging*. NY: Springer.

Haas, W., & Olson, P. (1983, November). *Family physicians and geriatrics*. Paper presented at the 1983 annual meeting of the Gerontological Society of America, San Francisco.

Hannon, J. (1980). Effects of a course on aging in a graduate nursing curriculum. *Journal of Gerontological Nursing, 6*, 604–615.

Harris, D., & Changas, P. (1994). Revision of Palmore's second Facts on Aging Quiz From a True-False to a multiple-choice format. *Educational Gerontology, 20*,741–754.

Harris, D., Changas, P., & Palmore, E. (1996). Palmore's first facts on aging quiz in a multiple-choice format. *Educational Gerontology, 22,* 575–589.

Harris, L. (1981). *Aging in the eighties*. Washington, DC: National Council on the Aging.

Harris, N. (1979). *Secondary-school home economics teachers' attitudes toward the aged and knowledge of aging*. Unpublished manuscript from College of Home Economics, Florida State University, Tallahassee, FL.

Hess, B., & Markson, E. (1995). Poverty. In G. Maddox (Ed.), *The encyclopedia of aging*. NY: Springer.

Hogue, C. (1995). In G. Maddox (Ed.), *The encyclopedia of aging*. NY: Springer.

Holtzman, J., & Toewe, C., & Beck, J. (1979). Specialty preference and attitudes toward the aged. *Journal of Family Practice, 9,* 667–672.

Holtzman, J., & Beck, J., (1979). Palmore's Facts on Aging Quiz: A reappraisal. *The Gerontologist, 19*, 116–120.

Holtzman, J., & Beck, J. (1981). Cognitive knowledge and attitudes toward the aged of dental and medical students. *Educational Gerontology, 6*, 195–207.

Huckstadt, A. (1983). Do nurses know enough about gerontology? *Journal of Gerontological Nursing, 9*, 392–396.

Iannone, J. (1986). *Relationship between long-term care nurses' attitude toward the elderly and their knowledge of gerontological nursing, age, number of years in long-term care nursing, and level of nursing preparation*. Unpublished manuscript.

Jeffrey, D. (1978, February 13). *Knowledge about aging among undergraduates and graduate students.* Unpublished letter to E. Palmore.

Johnson, J. (1986, December 19–20). What we need to know about aging and mental health. *USA Weekend*, p. 1.

Jones, V. (1993). Attitudes and knowledge level of nursing personnel toward elderly persons. M.S. Thesis at Russell Sage College.

Kabacoff, R., Shaw, I., Putnam, E., & Klein, H. (1983). Comparison of administrators and direct service workers in agencies dealing with the elderly. *Psychological Reports, 52*, 979–985.

Kahana, B. (1995). Isolation. In G. Maddox (Ed.), *The encyclopedia of aging.* NY: Springer.

Kahana, E. (1995). Institutionalization. In G. Maddox (Ed.), *The encyclopedia of aging*. NY: Springer.

Kahana, E., & Kiyak, H. (1984). Attitudes and behavior of staff in facilities for the aged. *Research on Aging, 6*, 395–416.

Kamrass, L., & Stevens, M. (1979, November). *Attitudes toward the aged and self-esteem among young adults*. Paper presented at the 32nd annual meeting of the Gerontological Society, Washington, DC.

Kausler, D. (1995). Memory and memory theory. In G. Maddox (Ed.), *The encyclopedia of aging*. NY: Springer.

Keller, M. (1986). *Misconceptions about aging among nurses*. Unpublished manuscript.

Klemmack, D. (1978). An examination of Palmore's FAQ. *The Gerontologist, 18*, 403–406.

Klemmack, D., & Roff, L. (1981). Predicting general and comparative support for government's providing benefits to older persons. *The Gerontologist, 21*, 592–599.

Klemmack, D., & Roff, L. (1983). Stimulus evaluation and the relationship between a deterministic cognitive system and cognitive differentiation. *The Journal of Psychology*, 113, 199–209.

Kline, T., & Kline, D. (1991a). The association between education, experience, and performance on two knowledge of aging and elderly questionnaires. *Educational Gerontology, 17,* 355–361.

Kline, D., Scialfa, C., Stier, D., & Babbitt, T. (1990). Effects of bias and educational experience on two knowledge of aging questionnaires. *Educational Gerontology, 16,* 297–310.

Knox, V., Gekoski, W., & Johnson, E. (1986). Contact with and perceptions of the elderly. *The Gerontologist, 26*, 309–313.

Kogan, N. (1961). Attitudes toward old people. *Journal of Abnormal Psychology, 62*, 44–54.

Koyano, W., Inoue, K., & Shibata, H. (1987). Negative misconceptions about aging in Japanese adults. *Journal of Cross-Cultural Gerontology, 2*, 131–137.

Kwan, A. (1982). *An examination of the validity of Palmore's Facts on Aging Quiz*. Unpublished abstract (Hong Kong).

Labouvie-Vief, G. (1985). Intelligence and cognition. In J. E. Birren & K. W. Schaie (Eds.), *Handbook of the psychology of aging* (2nd ed.) New York: Van Nostrand Reinhold.

Lakin, M. (1995). Psychotherapy. In G. Maddox (Ed.), *The encyclopedia of aging*. NY: Springer.

Laner, M. (1981). Palmore's FAQ: Does it measure learning? *Gerontology and Geriatrics Education, 2*, 3–7.

Larson, R. (1978). Thirty years of research on the subjective well-being of older Americans. *Journal of Gerontology, 40*, 109–129.

Lebowitz, B. (1995). Mental Health Services. In G. Maddox (Ed.), *The encyclopedia of aging*. NY: Springer.

Levenson, R. (1978, January 19). *Effects of a course in psychology on knowledge about aging among undergraduate students*. Unpublished letter to E. Palmore.

Levin, J. (1995). Religious organizations. In G. Maddox (Ed.), *The encyclopedia of aging*. NY: Springer.

Levy, W., & West, H. (1989). Knowledge of aging among clergy. *Journal of Religion & Aging, 5*(3), 67–74.

Levy, W., & West, H. (1985, October 19). *Knowledge of aging in human service professions*. Paper presented at the annual meeting of the Texas chapter, National Association of Social Workers, Dallas.

Light, B. (1978, December 5). *Knowledge of aging among students, nurses and residents of a nursing home*. Unpublished letter to E. Palmore.

Linn, B., & Zeppa, B. (1987). Predicting third year medical students' attitudes toward the elderly and treating the old. *Gerontology & Geriatrics Education, 7,* 167–175.

Linsk, N., & Pinkston, E. (1984). Training gerontological practitioners in home based family intervention. *Educational Gerontology, 10*, 289–305.

Lopata, H. (1995). Widowhood. In G. Maddox (Ed.), *The encyclopedia of aging*. NY: Springer.

Lusk, S., Williams, R., & Hsuing, S. (1990). An evaluation of the Facts on Aging Quizzes, *Journal of Nursing Education, 34,* 317–324.

Luszcz, M. (1982). Facts on aging: An Australian validation. *The Gerontologist, 22*, 369–372.

Luszcz, M., & Fitzgerald, K. (1986). Understanding cohort differences in cross-generational, self, and peer perceptions. *Journal of Gerontology, 41*, 234–240.

Mace, N., & Rabins, P. (1991). *The 36-hour day*. Baltimore: Johns Hopkins Press.

Maeda, D. (1981). Multivariate analysis of knowledge about old people and the sense of responsibility toward parents, in the case of urban middle-aged persons. *Social Gerontology, 12*, 3–5.

Manton, K. (1995). Long-term care survey. In G. Maddox (Ed.), *The encyclopedia of aging*. NY: Springer.

Massino, F. (1993). An analysis of variables related to students attitudes toward and knowledge of elderly persons. *Dissertation Abstracts International,* Vol. 54-05B, 2809.

Matthews, A., Tindale, J., & Norris, J. (1984). The FAQ: A Canadian validation and cross-cultural comparison. *Canadian Journal on Aging, 3,* 165–175.

McCutcheon, L. (1986). Development of the Psychological Facts on Aging Quiz. *Community/Junior College Quarterly, 10*, 123–129.

McDowell, J. (1978). *Factors related to misconceptions about aging among nurses*. Unpublished manuscript.

McKinlay, R. (1979a). *Knowledge about aging among graduate students in gerontology*. Unpublished table.

McKinlay, R. (1979b). *Knowledge about aging among the aged*. Unpublished tables.

McMillon, G. (1993). Aging: Knowledge and attitudes of vocational home economics teachers. *Dissertation Abstracts International, 54-11A,* 4010.

Meiburg, A. (1981). Knowledge of aging among clergy in Virginia. Unpublished letter to Palmore.

Miller, C. (1987). Patterns of factual knowledge and misconceptions about aging revealed by family members of the elderly in a long term care facility. Unpublished dissertation in the Department of Nursing, Mercy College, Yonkers, NY.

Miller, R., & Acuff, F. (1982). Stereotypes and retirement: A perspective from the Palmore FAQ. *Sociological Spectrum, 2*, 187–199.

Miller, R., & Dodder, R. (1980). A revision of Palmore's FAQ. *The Gerontologist, 20*, 673–679.

Miller, R., & Dodder, R. (1984). An empirical analysis of Palmore's FAQ and the Miller-Dodder revision. *Social Spectrum, 4*, 53–69.

Mishaan, M. (1992). The relationships among life satisfaction, level of activity, knowledge about aging, self-assessed health and perceived financial adequacy in a group of aged persons. *Dissertation Abstracts International, 53(1-A),* 262.

Mitty, E. (1995). Nursing Homes. In G. Maddox (Ed.), *The encyclopedia of aging*. NY: Springer.

Monk, A., & Kaye, L. (1982). Gerontological knowledge and attitudes of students of religion. *Educational Gerontology, 8*, 435–445.

Murdaugh, J. (1978, February 5). Knowledge of aging among geropsychiatric nurses. Unpublished letter to E. Palmore.

Murphy, R., Die, A., & Walker, J. (1986). Changing attitudes toward the elderly: The impact of three methods of attitude change. *Educational Gerontology, 12*, 241–251.

Myers, G. (1995). Demography. In G. Maddox (Ed.), *The encyclopedia of aging*. NY: Springer.

Myers, J., Weissman, M., Tischler, G., Holzer, C., Leaf, P., Orvaschel, H., Anthony, J., Boyd, J., Burke, J., Kramer, M., & Stoltzman, R. (1984). Six-month prevalence rates of psychiatric disorders in three communities. *Archives of General Psychiatry, 41*, 959–967.

National Center for Health Statistics. (1995). Current estimates from the National Health Interview Survey, 1994. *Vital & Health Statistics*, Series 10, No. 193.

National Safety Council. (1996). *Accident facts.* Chicago: National Safety Council.

Netting, F., & Kennedy, L. (1985). Project RENEW: Development of a volunteer respite care. *The Gerontologist, 25,* 573–583.

Neugarten, B., & Weinstein, K. (1964). The changing American grandparent. *Journal of Marriage and the Family, 26*, 266–273.

Noel, M., Ames, B. (1989). Attitudes, knowledge, and problem-solving approach of Michigan dietitians about aging. *Journal of American Dietetic Association, 89,* 1753–1757.

Norris, J., Tindale, J., & Matthews, A. (1987). The factor structure of the FAQ. *The Gerontologist, 27,* 673–676.

O'Hanlon, A., Camp, C., & Osofsky, H. (1993). Knowledge of and attitudes toward aging in middle aged, and older college students. *Educational Gerontology, 19,* 753–766.

Okama, V., & Johnson, J. (1986). Use of gerontological knowledge in the elementary classroom. *Nursing Homes, 35*, 22–25.

Okun, M. (1995). Subjective well-being. In G. Maddox (Ed.), *The encyclopedia of aging*. NY: Springer.

Palmore, E. (1976). The future status of the aged. *The Gerontologist, 16*, 297–302.

Palmore, E. (1977). Facts on aging: A short quiz. *The Gerontologist, 18*, 315–320.

Palmore, E. (1978). Professor Palmore responds. *The Gerontologist, 18*, 406.

Palmore, E. (1980). The Facts on Aging Quiz: A review of findings. *The Gerontologist, 20*, 669–672.

Palmore, E. (1981a) The Facts on Aging Quiz: 2. *The Gerontologist, 21*, 431–437.

Palmore, E. (1981b). Palmore responds. *The Gerontologist, 21*, 115–116.

Palmore, E. (1981c). *Social patterns in normal aging*. Durham, NC : Duke University Press.

Palmore, E. (1985). *The honorable elders revisited*. Durham, NC: Duke University Press.

Palmore, E. (1986). Trends in the health of the aged. *The Gerontologist, 26*, 298–302.

Palmore, E. (1988). Response to "The Factor Structure of the FAQ." Letter to the Editor in *The Gerontologist, 28,* 125–126.

Palmore, E. (1990). Corrections and comments on Kline's Knowledge of Aging and the Elderly quiz. *Educational Gerontology, 16*(6), 645–646.

Palmore, E. (1990). *Ageism.* NY: Springer.

Palmore, E. (1992). Knowledge about aging: What we know and need to know. *The Gerontologist, 32,* 149–150.

Palmore, E., Cleveland, W., Nowlin, J., Ramm, D., & Siegler, I. (1979). Stress and adaptation in later life. *Journal of Gerontology, 34*, 841–851.

Patwell, T. (1991). Attitudes toward and knowledge about the elderly among acute-care nursing staff. M.S. Research Paper, University of Wisconsin-Madison School of Nursing.

Perrotta, P., Perkins, D., Schimpfhauser, R., & Calkins, E. (1981). Medical student attitudes toward geriatric medicine and patients. *Journal of Medical Education, 56*, 478–483.

Peterson, D. (1995). Adult education. In G. Maddox (Ed.), *The encyclopedia of aging.* NY: Springer.

Pierce, R. (1995). Pulmonary System. In G. Maddox (Ed.), *The encyclopedia of aging.* NY: Springer.

Poon, L. (1995). In G. Maddox (Ed.), *The encyclopedia of aging.* NY: Springer.

Pruchno, R., & Smyer, M. (1983). Mental health problems and aging: A short quiz. *International Journal of Aging and Human Development, 17*, 123–140.

Pulliam, S., & Dancer, J. (1996). Performance on the Facts on Aging Quiz 2 by undergraduate and graduate students in communicative disorders. *Psychological Reports, 78,* 66.

Rabins, P., & Motts, Z. (1981). Changing staff attitudes encountered in establishing a psychogeriatric unit. *Hospital and Community Psychiatry, 32,* 729–730.

Ramon, P. (1986). *Knowledge about aging among nursing home staff.* Unpublished manuscript.

Ramoth, J. (1985, June 3). *Knowledge of aging among teacher education students.* Unpublished letter to E. Palmore.

Reisberg, B. (1995). Senile dementia. In G. Maddox (Ed.), *The encyclopedia of aging.* NY: Springer.

Rhodes, S. (1983). Age-related differences in work attitudes and behavior. *Psychological Bulletin, 93,* 328–367.

Richardson, C. (1993). Utilizing curriculum to effect a change in the attitudes, knowledge, and interactions of community college students with the elderly. *Dissertation Abstracts International, 54-10A,* 3845.

Riddick, C. (1985). The impact of an in-service educational program on the gerontological knowledge and attitudes of geriatric recreational service providers. *Educational Gerontology, 11,* 127–135.

Rix, S. (1995). In G. Maddox (Ed.), *The encyclopedia of aging.* NY: Springer.

Robertson, J. (1991). Knowledge of aging: A study of university students enrolled in introductory level psychology courses. Abstract of PhD Dissertation in Health Education, Southern Illinois University at Carbondale.

Romeis, J., & Sussman, M. (1980). Cross-cultural differences on the Facts on Aging Quiz. *Ageing and Society, 2,* 357–370.

Root, N. (1981). Injuries at work are fewer among older employees. *Monthly Labor Review, 104,* 30–34.

Rosencranz, H., & McNevin, T. (1969). A factor analysis of attitudes toward the aged. *The Gerontologist, 9,* 55–59.

Ross, M. (1983). Learning to nurse the elderly: Outcome measures. *Journal of Advanced Nursing, 8,* 373–378.

Rydman, L. (1986). *Knowledge of the aging process and the aged among clerical and technical health care workers.* Unpublished abstract for master's thesis, Health Sciences Center, University of Illinois at Chicago.

Sakata, S., & Okamoto, T. (1985). The attitude of caregivers toward their work with the aged in nursing homes and factors influencing that attitude. *Social Gerontology, 22,* 99–100 (published by Tokyo Metropolitan Institute of Gerontology).

Satterfield, M., Yasumara, K., & Goodman, G. (1984). Impact of an engineered physical therapy program for the elderly. *International Journal of Rehabilitation Research, 7*, 151–152.

Schiffman, S. (1995). Smell. In G. Maddox (Ed.), *The encyclopedia of aging*. NY: Springer.

Sheeley, E. (1979, January 22). *Knowledge of aging among nursing students*. Unpublished letter to E. Palmore.

Shenk, D., & Lee, J. (1995). Meeting the educational needs of service providers: Effects of a continuing education program on self-reported knowledge and attitudes about aging. *Educational Gerontology, 21,* 671–681.

Shock, N. (1985). Longitudinal studies of aging in humans. In C. Finch & E. Schneider (Eds.), *Handbook of the biology of aging*. New York: Van Nostrand Reinhold.

Singleton, J., Harbison, J., Melanson, P., Jackson, G. (1993). A study of the factual knowledge and common misperceptions about aging held by health care professionals. *Activities, Adaptation & Aging, 18,* 37–47.

Smith, M., Fincham, J., Ladner, K., & O'Quin, J. (1989). Mississippi Pharmacists' scores on the FAQ. *Journal of Geriatric Drug Therapy, 14,* 91–98.

Smith, M. (1985). *The changing attitudes of the physical therapy student toward the geriatric patient*. Unpublished manuscript.

Starr, B. (1995). Sexuality. In G. Maddox (Ed.), *The encyclopedia of aging*. NY: Springer.

Steinhauer, M., & Brockway, J. (1980). The impact of gerontological education: Knowledge and attitudes of public management students toward the elderly. In I. Wittels & J. Hendricks (Eds.), *Gerontology tomorrow: Consolidation/expansion*? Washington, DC: Association for Gerontology in Higher Education.

Steel, L. (1987). Dental students' attitudes and knowledge about elderly people. *Gerondontics, 3,* 61–64.

Strayer, M., DiAngelis, A., & Loupe, M. (1987). Ohio dentists' knowledge and perceptions of the elderly. *Ohio Dental Journal, 61,* 20–24.

Stone, V. (1977). *Knowledge of aging among undergraduate and faculty nurses*. Unpublished table.

Stum, M. (1993). Knowledge of aging of subsidized housing managers for the elderly: Implications for training. *Educational Gerontology, 19,* 127–138.

Sussman, M., Romeis, J., & Maeda, D. (1980). Age bias in Japan: Implications for normative conflict. *International Review of Modern Sociology, 10,* 243–254.

Swaykus, M. (1987). *Knowledge about aging and mental health among nurses and aides in nursing homes*. Unpublished table.

Tojo, M., & Maeda, D. (1985). Attitude of caregivers in nursing homes as measured by the Job Description Index. *Social Gerontology, 22*, 98–99 (published by Tokyo Metropolitan Institute of Gerontology).

Tonna, E. (1995). Musculoskeletal system. In G. Maddox (Ed.), *The encyclopedia of aging*. NY: Springer.

Tuckman, J., & Lorge, I. (1952). The effect of institutionalization on attitudes toward old people. *Journal of Abnormal Psychology, 47*, 337–344.

Tyson, S. (1992). The design, implementation and evaluation of a faculty development program in gerontological nursing. Ed.D. dissertation, NY City Technical College, City University of NY.

U.S. Bureau of Census. (1993). *Current population reports* (P25-1104). Washington: Government Printing Office.

U.S. Bureau of Census. (1996). *Statistical abstract of the U.S.* Washington: Government Printing Office.

U.S. Senate Special Committee on Aging. (1991). *Aging America: Trends and projections*. Washington: Government Printing Office.

Wallace, R. W., & Wallace, R. K. (1982). Assessing clergy's knowledge of aging: Suggestions for training. *Gerontology and Geriatrics Education, 2*, 285–290.

Walter, M. (1986). *Biases and misconceptions of nurses toward the elderly*. Unpublished manuscript.

West, H., & Ernst, M. (1981). The life enrichment program for older adults: An alternative educational model. *Educational Gerontology, 7*, 257–274.

West, H., & Levy, W. (1981). Knowledge of aging in an elderly population. *Research on Aging, 3*, 202–210.

West, H., & Levy, W. (1984). Knowledge of aging in the medical profession. *Gerontology and Geriatrics Education, 4*, 23–31.

Wexler, E. (1979, January 22). *Knowledge about aging among public health nurses*. Unpublished letter to E. Palmore.

Whanger, A. (1980). Nutrition, diet, and exercise. In E. Busse & D. Blazer (Eds.), *Handbook of geriatric psychiatry*. New York: Van Nostrand Reinhold.

Whittington, F. (1978). *Knowledge of aging among nursing students*. Unpublished table.

Wicker, C. (1995). Ageism and the American dream: The administration of the FAQ in a multicultural setting. Unpublished research project for the Masters of Social Work program at the University of Hawaii School of Social Work.

Wiener, J., Hanley, R., Clark, R. & van Nostrand, N. (1990). Measuring the activities of daily living. *Journal of Gerontology, 45*(6), S229–237.

Williams, A. (1982). *A comparison of attitudes toward aging between types of nurses*. Unpublished

Williams, R., Lusk, S., & Kline, N. (1986). Knowledge of aging and cognitive styles in baccalaureate nursing students. *The Gerontologist, 26*, 545–550.

Wilson, R., & Glamser, F. (1982). The impact of a gerontological intervention on osteopathic medical students. *Educational Gerontology, 8*, 373–380.

Wirth, J. (1987). Ageism: Predictors and trends (1980–1985). Paper prepared for the Gerontological Society of America Annual Meeting, Nov., 1987.

Wolk, M. (1986). *Gerontological knowledge of nursing students*. Unpublished manuscript.

Woodruff-Pak, D. (1995). Sleep. In G. Maddox (Ed.), *The encyclopedia of aging*. NY: Springer.

Youngman, B. (1980). *Clergy and nonclergy's beliefs and knowledge about old people*. Unpublished doctoral dissertation, Michigan State University.

Zigarmi, D. (1986). *Middle school students' attitudes toward the aged*. Unpublished manuscript.

Index